FELIX SANDBERG

*Und abends schlaf ich
mit nem Lächeln ein*

———

*At night I fall asleep
with a smile on my face*

Für meine Mutter Dorothee

For my mother Dorothee

Aus einer Karte von meinem Vater
zu meinem 31. Geburtstag:

*Gehe deinen Weg wie ein Wanderer,
der einen anstrengenden Weg bergauf geht,
aber mit jedem Schritt immer mehr sieht.*

Lieber Papa,

vielen Dank für deine
uneingeschränkte Unterstützung!

———

From a card my father
gave to me for my 31st birthday:

*Go your way like a hiker following
an uphill path to be rewarded with a
better view the higher he gets.*

Dear Dad,

thank you so much
for your unconditional support!

Liebe Leserin und lieber Leser,

schön, dass du mein Buch in die Hand genommen und diese Seite aufgeschlagen hast. Offensichtlich hat es dich auf irgendeine Weise angesprochen. Das freut mich und ich hoffe, dass du es so schnell nicht wieder aus der Hand gibst.

Wir alle stellen uns immer wieder diese Fragen, obwohl wir eigentlich wissen, dass wir sie nicht beantworten können. Fragen über Liebe und Leben, über Glück und die Zukunft und so weiter und über all die wichtigen Dinge drum herum, die meist keine Dinge sind. *Was mache ich mit meinem Leben? Ist jene Entscheidung besser als eine andere? Wen liebe ich oder nicht? Was ist richtig, was ist falsch? Was definiert unser Zusammenleben?* Und so weiter. Die Liste ist lang. Viele dieser Fragen stellt sich die Menschheit schon seit ihrem Bestehen.

Ich für mich bezweifle, dass ich sie beantworten kann. Schon zu viele große Köpfe sind an ihnen gescheitert. Und so entstand bei mir aus einem Gefühl der Leere ein Commitment zum Moment über den Plan, zum Finden statt einer Suche. Ich schärfte meine Wahrnehmung und steigerte das Bewusstsein für mein Umfeld. Dies führt immer wieder zu Ideen, die ich in Objekte verwandle und zunehmend entstehen daraus auch Fotografien als Träger konzeptueller Gedanken. Vielleicht klingt das alles etwas abstrakt, aber im Laufe des Buches wird diese Beschreibung sicherlich greifbarer.

Doch viele unverwirklichte Ideen schlummern in meinem Archiv, wunderschöne Bilder, die kaum jemand zu Gesicht bekommen hat, liegen tief vergraben in digitalen Lagern und auch mein Handy ist voller ungenutzter Notizen. Oft sind es Sammlungen spontaner Gedanken, Beobachtungen meines Umfeldes oder Erfahrungen aus meinem kreativen Tun. Ab und zu sind es auch Geschichten, entstanden aus Gesprächen, die ich zufällig mithörte, zum Beispiel im Café oder im Nachtbus um halb vier.

Allesamt halte ich sie für zu schade, um sie für mich zu behalten. Ich möchte sie teilen. Wenn ich für all diese Gedanken aktuell keine Verwendung oder auf die Fragen keine Antworten habe, vielleicht haben das ja andere, dachte ich mir.

Und plötzlich passten Gedanken zu Bildern und die Bilder zueinander. Ich stellte sie gegenüber oder arrangierte sie neu. Was noch nicht da war, entstand bald darauf auf unzähligen Streifzügen durch meine Wahlheimat Berlin. Oft fotografierte ich einfach Szenen, die mich ansprachen, und erkannte erst später ihren Zusammenhang mit einem anderen Bild oder Text. Mit wenigen Ausnahmen ist nichts in diesem Buch gestellt. Alles ist einfach so passiert und fügte sich, wie von magischer Hand geleitet, zusammen. Innerhalb kürzester Zeit war das Buch geboren.

Worum geht es bei deinem Buch?, werde ich noch während des Erstellens gefragt. Eine Antwort bleibe ich schuldig und ziehe mich zurück in das Chaos meiner Arbeit. Da erkenne ich: Dies ist der Inhalt meines Buches. Es ist ein Spaziergang durch das Chaos in meinem Kopf, durch meine chaotische Gedankenwelt – ohne Ordnung. Wie bei einem echten Spaziergang folgt ein Bildeindruck einem nächsten: hier ein verliebtes Pärchen, dort fällt ein Blatt vom Baum. Was davor geschah, bleibt uns verborgen. Wir können für einen kurzen Moment verweilen, beobachten und unseren Gedanken freien Lauf lassen. Oder wir gehen weiter und sind sogleich inmitten eines neuen Schauplatzes, dem Schauplatz auf der nächsten Seite.

So steht jede Doppelseite für sich. Manchmal unterstreicht das Bild den Inhalt, manchmal ist es aber einfach nur ein schönes Bild neben einem Gedanken. Ab und an sind es zwei Bilder, die zusammen für mich ein Thema abbilden oder einfach gemeinsam wunderschön sind. Ungeordnet stehen sie hintereinander. Aus dieser Unordnung kann Neues entstehen – bei mir oder noch besser beim Leser und Betrachter.

Die meisten Gedanken fasste ich auf Deutsch. Doch ab und an entstanden diese während englischsprachigen Unterhaltungen. Eine analoge deutsche Übersetzung empfand ich manchmal als nicht ganz treffend. In diesen Fällen sind die Texte nur in Englisch zu finden.

Sicherlich kommen neue Fragen auf: *Wo ist dieses Foto entstanden? Was meint er genau mit jener Aussage?* Nicht alles wird erläutert, aber ab S. 272 sind zusätzliche Informationen zu Bildern und Erklärungen zu einzelnen Aussagen zu finden.

Was den Inhalt in diesem Buch vereint, ist der Blick eines neugierigen Menschen, der mit offenen Augen durch die Welt geht, den Moment lebt, vieles sieht und manches hört, sich dafür begeistert und abends mit nem Lächeln einschläft.

Felix Sandberg   Berlin, im Sommer und Herbst 2018

Dear reader,

I'm glad you picked up my book and landed on this page. Obviously, it appealed to you in some way. This makes me happy and I hope you won't put it down again anytime soon.

We all keep asking ourselves these questions, even though we know that we don't actually have the answers. Questions about love and life, about happiness, the future and so on; and about all the other important things in life that mostly aren't things. *What am I doing with my life? Should I go with that decision or the other one? Who do I love or not love? What is right, what is wrong? What determines the way we live together?* And all the rest of it. It's a long list. These questions are as old as mankind itself.

I doubt that I'm able to come up with the answers. After all, countless great minds attempted to accomplish this task and failed. And thus, driven by a feeling of emptiness, I opted to commit to the moment instead to a plan, to finding instead of searching. I honed my perception and started to pay more attention to the world surrounding me. Time and again this heightened awareness triggers ideas, which I turn into objects, and increasingly into photographs as a medium of conceptual thoughts. This may sound a little too abstract but in the course of the book this description should become more tangible.

Still, there are many unrealized ideas lying dormant in my archive. Beautiful pictures hardly anyone has ever seen are buried deep in digital storage and my cell phone holds a wealth of unexploited notes. The latter frequently comprise collections of spontaneous thoughts, written down observations of my surroundings or experiences arising from my creative work. At times, these stories originate from conversations I overheard by accident, e.g. in a coffee shop or on a night bus at half past three.

I like to think that all of these stories are too good to keep to myself. I want to share them. So I said to myself: even if I currently don't have any use for these reflections or don't have any answers to these questions, maybe others do.

And all of a sudden, thoughts complemented pictures and pictures each other. I juxtaposed or rearranged them. What didn't exist yet soon materialized on one of my countless outings in my adopted hometown of Berlin. I would often simply photograph scenes that appealed to me and only later recognize their link with another image or piece of text. With a few exceptions, nothing in this book was staged. Everything just sort of happened and came together as if by magic. In a very short period of time the book was born.

What is your book about? people ask while I'm still in the process of writing. I fail to reply, retreat into the chaos that comes with my work and then realize: this is the topic of my book. It is a walk through the chaos in my head, through my chaotic world of ideas – completely at random. Just like on a real walk, one visual impression follows another: here's a couple in love, over there a leaf falls off a tree. What happened earlier remains hidden. We can linger for a short while, observe and let our minds wander. Or, we keep walking and immediately enter a new scene, the scene on the next page.

Each double spread stands alone. Occasionally, the image will emphasize the written content, while elsewhere it is just a beautiful picture sitting next to an embodied thought. Now and then two images are placed next to each other because, to me, they depict a certain theme or simply look beautiful that way. The sequence follows no particular order. This disorder can give birth to something new – within me, or, even better yet, within the reader and viewer.

New questions are likely to arise: *Where was this photo taken? What exactly does he mean by that?* Since not everything is spelled out you can find additional information and explanations regarding the pictures and individual statements from page 282 onwards.

While most of the captured thoughts originally occurred to me in German, some emerged during conversations in English. To make the book's content accessible to everyone I decided to translate all text passages into English. But some pages simply didn't offer enough room to place text in both languages and a picture. In these cases I decided to move the English text to the back of the book in order to keep the design as clean as possible and insert a reference to the page containing the translation.

The leitmotif of this book's content is a curious person's gaze; it follows a person who takes in the world with his eyes wide open, lives in the moment, sees many and hears some things, who is enthusiastic about all of it and at night falls asleep with a smile on his face.

Felix Sandberg	Berlin, summer and autumn 2018

Ich bin auf diese Erde
gekommen und irgendwann
muss ich wieder gehen.

Diese Zeit nennen wir Leben.

Es liegt an mir, was ich
mit dieser Zeit anstelle.

———

I came into this world
and some day
I will have to leave it.

This period of time we call life.

It's up to me how
I will use that time.

Ja, manchmal
ist das Leben ein
Kampf.

Aber es macht
auch einfach sehr
viel Spaß.

———————

Yes, sometimes
life
is a struggle.

But it's
also
a lot of fun.

Schlangen
sind
verführerisch.

―――――

Snakes
are
seductive.

Ein mexikanischer
Botschafter
erklärte einst seinem Sohn:

*Glaube nur die Hälfte
von dem, was du siehst.*

*Glaube nichts von dem,
was du hörst.*

———

A Mexican
ambassador once told
his son:

*Of what you see:
believe half.*

*Of what you hear:
believe nothing.*

Die Eulen
haben ihr Nest
bezogen.

———

The owls
are
nesting.

Berlin

Shanghai

In China essen sie Hunde.
Wir glauben, das ist falsch.

Wir essen Kühe. Ein Hindu
glaubt, das ist eine Todsünde.

———

In China they eat dogs.
We think that's wrong.

We eat cows. A Hindu believes
that to be a mortal sin.

There
is never
just
one way.

Weißt du,
wie schön
Licht und Schatten
sein können?

―――――

Are you aware
of the beauty
of light
and shadow?

Ich sitze in der U-Bahn, neben mir ein Vater mit seiner Tochter. In einem Moment stellt er schockiert fest: Die Hose seiner Tochter hat Flecken. Er spricht sie darauf an: *Warum hast du denn die Hose mit den Flecken angezogen?* Sie antwortet darauf: *Die Flecken erinnern mich an all die schönen Dinge, die ich erlebt habe.*

Entdecke die Welt mit den Augen eines Kindes!

———

I'm on the subway sitting next to a father and his daughter. He's appalled when he suddenly realizes: his daughter's pants are stained. He asks her: *Why are you wearing this dirty pair of pants?* She replies: *The stains remind me of all the nice things that have happened to me.*

See the world through the eyes of a child!

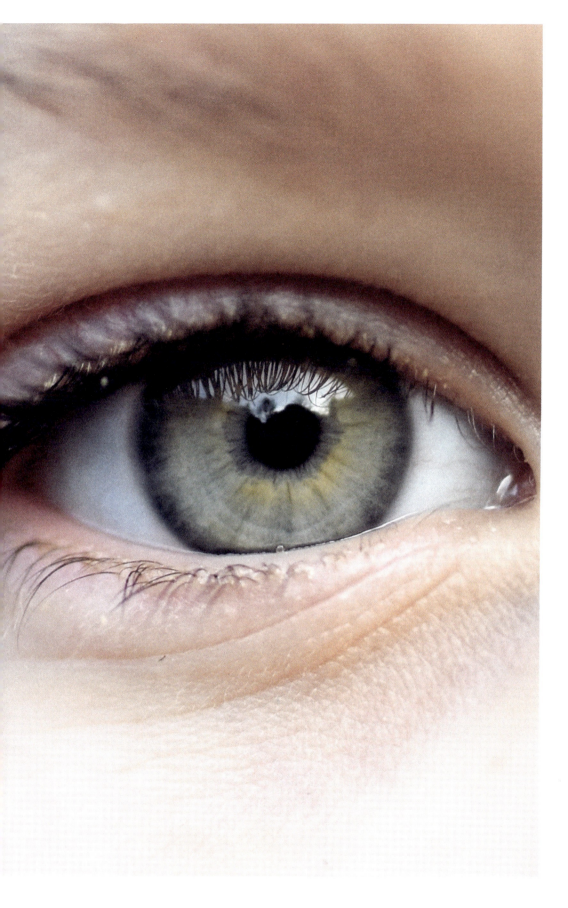

Wie würdest du einen
Halbmond malen?

Vielleicht sieht er anders
aus, als du denkst.

Aber wie sieht ein
richtiger Halbmond aus?

How would you paint
a half moon?

Maybe it looks nothing
like you think.

But what does a *proper*
half moon look like?

Sei Paradiesvogel
oder nicht.
Aber sei du selbst.

———

Be a bird of paradise
or not.
But be yourself.

Ich habe mir ein Bild gekauft
von einem Künstler, den ich sehr bewundere.
Bis heute kann ich es stundenlang betrachten.
Es bewegt mich immer noch sehr.

Die einzige Frage, die ich von anderen gestellt
bekomme, ist: *Wie viel hat es gekostet?*

―――――

I bought a painting from an artist
I admire very much. To this day, I enjoy
looking at it for hours on end. It still
moves me deeply.

The only question I get asked by
others is: *How much did it cost?*

Don't get blinded
by the light.

Ich stehe in einer kleinen Galerie in der sich rasant verändernden Potsdamer Straße in Berlin. Die Galerie ist gut gefüllt an diesem Tag, es herrscht reges Treiben, Interessierte kommen und gehen. Zentral im Raum sitzt der Galerist auf einem Designerstuhl aus der Mitte des letzten Jahrhunderts. Zurückgelehnt hat er die Arme hinter seinem Kopf verschränkt und weist mit klarer und bestimmter Stimme seine attraktive Assistentin ein: *Das bitte alles machen!* Er macht eine kurze gedankliche Pause. *Und ansonsten – einfach auskennen. Auskennen ist ganz wichtig! Damit du dich auskennst! Und wenn was nicht klappt, meldet ihr euch, damit ich euch Geld rüberschiebe.* Ein Herr verabschiedet sich und ruft quer durch den Raum: *Also wir gehen dann später noch in ne Bar.* Der Galerist in einer Mischung aus Interesse und Verdutztheit: *In welche Bar?* Der Gast antwortet ihm, indem er langsam jede einzelne Silben betont: *Die Vic-to-ria Bar.* Darauf der Galerist in einer ruhigen, fast verträumten Stimme: *Ich glaube, von Bars halte ich mich heute fern.*

I'm standing in a small gallery in the rapidly changing Potsdamer Strasse in Berlin. The gallery is rather busy today, there is a lively atmosphere with interested parties coming and going. The gallery owner is sitting in the center of the room in a mid-century designer chair. Leaning back with his arms crossed behind his head, he instructs his attractive assistant in a clear and determined voice: *Please take care of all of that!* He takes a moment to think. *And other than that – know the ropes. Knowing the ropes is very important! So you know what's what! And in case something goes wrong just let me know, so I can send you some money.* A man says goodbye and calls out across the room: *We'll go to some bar later.* The gallery owner sounds both interested and bewildered: *Which bar?* The guest answers, slowly stressing every single syllable: *The Vic-to-ria Bar.* To which the gallery owner replies in a quiet, almost dreamy voice: *I think I'll stay away from bars today.*

Die Erschaffung
der
Technologie.

———

The creation
of
technology.

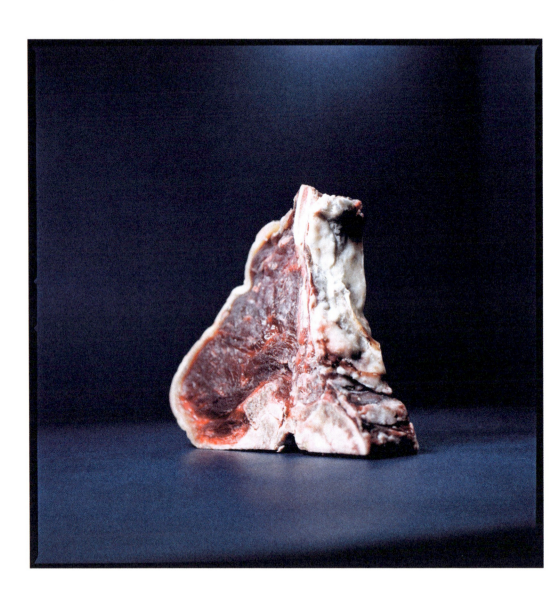

SUPERMODEL Claudia

Das Unvollkommene macht
einen Körper vollkommen.
Zu jeder Zeit.

Imperfectly perfect.
At all times.

Kind oder Kunst?

———

Child or art?

Ich bin auf einer Vernissage im erhabenen Stadtviertel Charlottenburg, ein feines Pflaster. Ungewöhnlich, aber Preislisten sind im Umlauf. Die Herrschaften stehen umher und vergnügen sich an den ausgedruckten Stücken Papier. Eine Dame schaut einem älteren Herrn über die Schulter. Er hält sein Weißweinglas und die Preisliste in ein und derselben Hand. Mit der anderen Hand blättert er die Seiten vor und zurück. Da bemerkt er die Dame: *Wollen sie mal?*, fragt er in ihre Richtung. *Ach ne, passt schon, ich wollte nur mal schauen,* antwortet die Dame leicht peinlich berührt. *Ja ich schaue auch nur,* meint der Herr. *Ach so,* antwortet die Dame schmunzelnd. Auch der Herr schmunzelt jetzt. Gemeinsam stehen sie nun vor einem der ausgestellten Bilder und blättern die vier Seiten mehrere Male vor und zurück. Ein Blick auf das Gemälde, dann wieder in die Preisliste, als wäre es so schwer das ausgestellte Bild zu finden … *Ah da ist es ja.*

Zahlen ohne inhaltlichen Bezug, Preise ohne Bezug zur Realität. Nach einiger Zeit sehe ich in den Händen der umherstehenden Kunst-Bourgeoisie die mittlerweile vom Schweiß ihrer Hände gewellten Preislisten, an den Kanten der Papiere, in der Mitte, da wo ihre Hände am meisten hinkommen, sind sie deutlich gefärbt vom Schmutz der edlen Griffe. Nun schmunzle ich über diese wundervolle Beobachtung, in meinen Augen vielleicht auch ein bisschen Kunst, und ich denke mir: Kreativer Ungehorsam ist etwas Wundervolles.

I'm at an exhibition opening in the superior Charlottenburg district in Berlin, a posh area. Though unusual, price lists are being circulated. The elegant visitors are having fun with the printouts. One lady peeks over the shoulder of an elderly gentleman. He's holding his white wine glass and the price list in the same hand. With his other hand he's flipping the pages back and forth. Then he notices the lady: *Would you like the list?* he asks in her direction. *Oh, no, that's okay, I just wanted to take a look,* the lady replies slightly embarrassed. *Yes, of course, I am also just browsing,* the man says. *Ah, I see,* the lady answers with a smile. The gentleman seems amused as well. Both are now standing in front of one of the paintings and keep flipping the four pages back and forth. They study the painting, then look back at the price list, as if it were really difficult to find the picture on display … *Ah, there it is.*

Random figures, prices out of touch with reality. After a while, I notice that the price lists in the hands of the art bourgeoisie are curling from the sweat of their palms. On the edges and in the middle of the sheets where their hands touch them the most, they are now stained from the dirt of their exquisite fingers. This wonderful observation makes me smile. In my view, this might also constitute some kind of art and I think to myself: creative disobedience is something wonderful.

The invasion
of space.

Sadly inverted.

Goodbye

Berlin, Oranienburger Straße. In unmittelbarer Nähe des Kottbusser Tores gelegen, ist sie eine ikonische Straße. Kurz hinter der ehemaligen Grenze zu Ostberlin war sie einst das Herz der Berliner Hausbesetzerszene, zu einer Zeit, als es noch etwas zu besetzen gab. Nebenbei türkische Einkaufsstraße, ist sie heute eher Fressgasse für Touristen. Ich bin neu in Berlin und auf Entdeckungsreise durch die Stadt. Ein Geschäft sticht heraus. Es sieht anders aus als die anderen. Ich gehe darauf zu. Am Türrahmen lehnt in lässiger Manier ein adrett gekleideter Herr. Er trägt eine weite Baumwollhose und einen Panama-Hut. Als er sieht, dass seine Auslage mein Interesse geweckt hat, ruft er sofort in einem für Altberliner typisch schroffen Ton: *Komm rein!* Es ist der Künstler Klaus Theuerkauf. Last Man Standing – seit Anfang der Achtzigerjahre betreibt er hier die Produzentengalerie *endart*. Ich trete ein und sofort beginnt er zu erzählen:

Seit dreißig Jahren bin ich hier. Auch wenn ich aktuell 4700 Euro Mietschulden habe. Aber mein Vermieter hat dafür Verständnis. Er ist auch Kunstsammler. Für 800 000 Mark hat er das Haus damals gekauft. Heute ist er ein in Berlin bekannter Gastronom. Die PDS hat es damals möglich gemacht. Auch ein Spitzenpolitiker der Grünen hat sich ein Haus einige Meter weiter gekauft. Alle haben sich damals bedient. Ich hätte ja auch eines genommen, aber mir wollten sie ja keines geben. Er redet am laufenden Band, von damals, von heute, von sich und über die anderen. Er zeigt mir seine Küche. Alles ist voll mit Kunst. Vieles aus einer andern Zeit und mit bitterbösem Humor. Darunter ein Rotkreuzkasten an der Wand, den er mit der Aufschrift versah: *Mit freundlichen Grüßen von Josef Mengele.*

Er erzählt von Jonathan Meese und dessen Gönner Herbert Volkmann. Mit Volkmann (damals noch mittellos) habe er selbst in den Achtzigerjahren Performances gemacht. Doch dann hätte dieser geerbt und sich daraufhin nicht mehr gemeldet, dafür aber den ganzen Kunstmarkt von Hirst bis Emin leergekauft. Er nimmt einen herumliegenden Ausstellungskatalog und zeigt mir die Bilder. *Die ganze Saatchi Gallery hat er leer gekauft. Klar, natürlich ist er ein Kokser. Sieht man sofort,* an seinen Bildern. *Ist er aber schon immer gewesen. Von den fünf Mal, die ich gekokst habe, habe ich es drei Mal mit ihm getan. Realistisch malen kann er natürlich. Das muss man ihm schon lassen. Aber, dass er immer diese Nutten und das Koks malen muss, mit Dollarscheinen und so. Abscheulich ist das.* Er zeigt mir ein weiteres Bild: *Selbstportrait mit Meese.*

Er will, dass ich seine Freundin besuche. Sie ist Modedesignerin. Ich könnte doch das ganze Marketing und so übernehmen. Da könne sie sich echt nicht drauf konzentrieren. *Komm, wir gehen in den Keller.* Dieser ist ebenfalls voll mit Kunstgegenständen, Skulpturen, Malerei, Dinge, undefinierbar. Viel habe er gemacht in all den Jahren. Er kramt in den Sachen. *Vielleicht entdecken sie mich ja noch.* Er zeigt mir seinen Weihnachtsmann. Es ist eine kleine Puppe, gekleidet als Weihnachtsmann. *Siehst du die Augen?* Er hat sie so übermalt, dass der Weihnachtsmann eine kristallblaue Iris mit stecknadelkopfgroßer

Pupille besitzt. Mit begeisterter Stimme erklärt er mir: *Das ist ein Stecki! Ganz klar.* Er kramt eine Spritze hervor und gibt sie ihm in die Hand. Wieder begeistert: *Siehst du das? Ganz klar, ein Stecki!* Am Gürtel des Weihnachtsmannes hängt ein Schild mit der Aufschrift *Kottbusser Tor,* der ehemalige Drogenumschlagplatz Nummer eins.

Jeder Mensch ist nützlich!, philosophiert er. *Selbst der Unnütze, der kann wenigstens als schlechtes Beispiel herangezogen werden.*

Mittlerweile schreibt Klaus seine Autobiografie. Darum erzählt er so viel. Weil er muss sich ja erinnern. *Morgens Steine, abends Kunst und Weine,* hat er damals immer gesagt. Er lässt Namen am laufenden Band fallen, immer mit der Bemerkung: *Kennste ja, ne?!* Ich habe die alle noch nie gehört und antworte mit *ja.* Er schenkt sich ein Glas Rotwein ein. Es ist 11:30 Uhr.

Seit 2015 befindet sich in seinen ehemaligen Galerieräumen ein türkischer Friseur mit Kronleuchter an der Decke. Das Haus gehört mittlerweile einem niederländischen Konsortium. Verkauft wurde es für ein Vielfaches des damaligen Preises.

Berlin, Oranienburger Strasse. It's an iconic street in close proximity to the Kottbusser Tor. Situated right behind the former border with East Berlin, it used to be the heart of Berlin's squat scene, at a time when there was still something to occupy. Though the street is also lined with Turkish shops, its present-day popularity with tourists can mostly be attributed to the countless eateries on offer. I am new to Berlin and exploring the city. One shop stands out. It looks different. I walk toward it. A well-dressed gentleman is casually leaning against the doorframe. He is wearing wide cotton trousers and a Panama hat. When he notices that his display has garnered my interest, he immediately calls out: *Come in!* in the brusque manner typical for an old-school Berliner. It is the artist Klaus Theuerkauf. Last Man Standing – he has been running the producer gallery *endart* here since the early eighties. I enter and he immediately starts talking:

I've been here for thirty years, even though I currently owe €4700 in rent. But my landlord is understanding. He is also an art collector. Back then he bought the house for 800,000 Deutsche Mark. Today he is a well-known restaurateur in Berlin. The PDS (former East German party) made it possible. (Note: he is referring to the time after the wall came down when the German government sold a lot of real estate in the former eastern part of the country way below its [true] value). *Even a top politician of the Green Party bought a house not far from here. Everybody helped themselves back then. I would have taken a property, too, but they didn't want me to have one.* He doesn't stop talking, about then, about today, about himself and about others. He shows me his kitchen, which is full of art. Most of it from a time gone by and depicting scathing humor; like a wall-mounted Red Cross box with the inscription: *With kind regards from Josef Mengele.*

He talks about Jonathan Meese and his patron, Herbert Volkmann. Together with Volkmann (penniless at that time) he had made performance art in the eighties. But after the patron had received an inheritance he never got in touch again; instead he went on to buy up the entire art market from Hirst to Emin. He picks up an exhibition catalog and shows me the paintings. *He stripped the Saatchi Gallery bare. Sure, of course, he's a cokehead. You can tell just by looking at his pictures. But then again, he always was. Of the five times I snorted blow, three times I did it with him. He knows how to paint realistically, no doubt about it. You've got to hand it to him. But why does he always have to paint hookers and coke, with dollar bills and other stuff. That's disgusting.* He shows me another painting: *Self-portrait with Meese.*

He wants me to visit his girlfriend. She is a fashion designer. He suggests I take over her marketing etc. since she really doesn't have time for that. *Come on, let's go down to the basement.* It is also bursting with works of art, sculptures, paintings, objects, indescribable. He says he has worked a lot in all these years and rummages about. *Maybe they'll discover me one day.* He shows me his Santa Claus. It's a little doll dressed as Santa. *Do you see the eyes?* He has painted over them to give his Santa crystal blue irises with pinhead-sized pupils. Sounding enthusiastic he explains: *That's a junkie! Obviously.* He digs out a syringe and puts it in the doll's hand. Again excited: *Do you see that? Obviously, a junkie!* There's a sign attached to Santa's belt with the inscription reading *Kottbusser Tor,* the former hotbed of drug trafficking.

Everyone is useful! he philosophizes. *Even the useless, at least they can serve as a bad example.*

Meanwhile, Klaus has started writing his autobiography. That's why he talks so much. Because he needs to remember things. *Street fights in the morning, enjoy art and wine in the evening* he used to say. He keeps dropping names nonstop, always remarking, *you know them, right?!* I've never heard of any of them and say yes. He pours himself a glass of red wine. It is 11:30 am.

In 2015, his former gallery space was turned into a Turkish barber's shop with chandeliers hanging from the ceiling. Nowadays a Dutch consortium owns the house. It sold for a multiple of the original purchase price.

In Berlin übernehmen
die Kidz.

_____

In Berlin the Kidz are
taking over.

Schön war's.

STAR WARS

Im Flugzeug. Der Herr auf dem Sitz vor mir tippt hastig auf seinem Laptop. Er trägt ein zu weit geschnittenes Hemd, wie damals in den Achtzigern modern, und dazu goldene Manschettenknöpfe. Das touristische Ehepaar neben mir empört sich über das langsame Bodenpersonal und entdeckt im Bordmagazin, dass ein Espresso nach dem Essen Kalorien verbrennen kann. Die Oma diagonal vor mir beschwert sich über die anderen Fluggäste und ihr schweres Gepäck. Mit wem sie spricht, bleibt mir verborgen. Ich schaue aus dem Fenster und sehe die Wolken, die wie Wattebäusche dicht aneinandergedrückt sind. Ich spüre die Kraft der Sonne, ich sehe den Horizont, die Schönheit der Unendlichkeit. Ich sehe, wie sich das Licht in den Seen und den Flüssen am Boden spiegelt. Ich sehe die unendliche Schönheit der Welt von oben und denke an die unbegrenzten Möglichkeiten. Ich sehe die Wiesen, die Straßen, die Häuser. Sehe Autobahnen, die in ästhetischen Schlingen die Felder teilen, die von Menschen geschaffenen Strukturen, diese wunderbaren Formen. Ich sehe was, was ihr nicht seht.

On a plane. The gentleman in the seat in front of me is hastily typing on his laptop keyboard. He's wearing an oversized eighties' shirt with golden cuff links. The tourist couple next to me is voicing its outrage over the slow ground crew and in the inflight magazine they discover that drinking an espresso after a meal can burn calories. The granny seated diagonally in front of me is complaining about the other passengers and their heavy luggage. I can't make out who she is speaking to. Looking out of the window I see clouds tightly pressed together like cotton balls. I feel the power of the sun; I see the horizon, the beauty of infinity. I see the light being reflected in the lakes and rivers on the ground. I see the infinite beauty of the world from above and think about the unlimited possibilities. I see the meadows, the streets, the houses. See looping highways aesthetically partition fields, man-made structures, such wonderful shapes. I spy with my little eye.

Das Wichtigste im Leben
ist wach zu sein.

Doch ein kleines Schläfchen
von Zeit zu Zeit ist Gold wert.

———————

The most important thing
in life is to be awake.

But a little nap now and
then is priceless.

Ich sitze an der Bar und schaue auf die andere Seite. Dort sitzt ein junges blondes Mädchen. Ihre Brüste sind groß. Nicht zu groß. Angenehm groß. Sie trägt einen Dutt. Einen großen Dutt. Keinen zu großen Dutt. Er ist angenehm groß. Würde ich ihn öffnen, gingen ihre Haare bis zum Po. Das glaube ich zumindest. Oder stelle es mir vor. Ich schaue sie an. Sie erwidert meine Blicke. Wieder und wieder. Mir ist es nahezu unmöglich, sie nicht anzusprechen. Mir steigt der Geruch von Frische in die Nase. Der Geruch von Minze. Von Gurke. Es sind die hippen Mixturen der Zeit. Der Großstadt. Der Bars der Großstadt. Ihre Blicke betteln danach, angesprochen zu werden. Ihre Blicke betteln nach mir. Ihre Seele bettelt nach mir. Ihr Herz – vermutlich alleine. Ich drehe mich beiseite. Schaue wieder zu ihr. Sie ist verschwunden.

Ich hätte zu ihr rübergehen können. Dann hätte ich mich neben sie an den Tresen gestellt, kurz abgewartet und mich dann langsam zu ihr gedreht. Ich hätte zu ihr sagen können: Ich saß bis eben noch auf der anderen Seite des Tresens und ich hatte mehrfach das Gefühl, dass sich unsere Blicke trafen. Es waren tiefe Blicke. Sie hätte geantwortet, dass das gut sein könne. Und ich darauf, dass mir das gefiel. Es waren intime Momente. Trotz der Großstadt und all der Menschen um uns herum. Das alles hätte ich tun können, doch ich tat es nicht.

Die Bar an einem Sonntagabend in einer Großstadt ist so dicht gefüllt, es gibt kaum einen Platz. Und trotzdem ist sie voller Einsamkeit.

I'm sitting at the bar looking across to the other side. A young blond girl is sitting there. Her breasts are big. Not too big. Pleasantly big. She is wearing her hair in a bun. A big bun. Not too big. It is pleasantly big. If I undid it, her hair would reach down to her buttocks. At least I think so. Or imagine it to be. I look at her. She returns my gaze. Again and again. It is almost impossible not to get up and speak to her. A scent of freshness wafts up my nose. The smell of fresh mint and cucumber. It's the flavor of the hip drinks of our time. It's the smell of the big cities. Of the bars in the big cities. Her glances implore me to talk to her. Her eyes are begging for me. Her soul is begging for me. Her heart – probably lonely. I turn away. Then look back in her direction. She is gone.

I could have joined her. I would have positioned myself beside her at the bar. I would have hesitated a moment and then slowly turned to her. I could have said: I was sitting on the other side of the bar and several times felt our eyes meet. Those were some pretty intense gazes. She would have answered that it might have been the case. And I would have said that I liked it. Those were intimate moments. Despite being in a big city and surrounded by a big crowd. I could have done all of that but I didn't.

The bar on a Sunday night in a big city is very crowded, there is hardly any place left. Nevertheless it is filled with loneliness.

I'm feeling so
connected.

Tinderama

Mein kürzestes Tinder-Date dauerte keine vier Minuten, bestand weitestgehend aus warten und hat zwei Euro gekostet. Die An- und Abreise von zusammen 43 Minuten sind da noch nicht eingerechnet. Dafür gab es ein paar flambierte Rippchen gratis. Sie waren übrig. Es war der Rest. Mein Date hatte sie gegrillt. Sie waren sehr gut.

Match.

Hey! Bist du der Hitze gut entflohen?, schreibe ich sie an, denn heute ist ein sehr heißer Tag. Sie: *Nein ich muss arbeiten. Hast du Lust später vorbeizukommen?*

Diese spontane Einladung überfordert mich. Nach einer ausgedehnten Radtour liege ich kraftlos auf der Couch und kann mir nicht vorstellen, eine Frau zu begeistern. Nicht mal verbal. Ich frage sie, was denn ihre Arbeit sei und sie antwortet, sie brate Fritten und Rippchen. Heute arbeitet sie bei den Fritten. Na das sind doch mal tolle Aussichten, denke ich mir. Und sie schreibt, dass ich es mir ja überlegen könne. Das tue ich und sage ihr ab. Müdigkeit, Zweifel und Bequemlichkeit gewinnen die Oberhand. Doch interessiert bin ich schon und so versuche ich sie am nächsten Tag zu einem Treffen zu überreden. Sie arbeitet schon wieder. Dieses Mal bei den Rippchen. Ich soll vorbeischauen. Mir schießen die Gedanken durch den Kopf. Ein Date am Grill? Was macht sie da genau? Kann ich mich da mit ihr unterhalten? Und wie stellt sie sich wohl ein gemeinsames Treffen zum Feierabend vor? Nach acht Stunden hinter rauchenden Kohlen wird ein deutlicher Grillgeruch nicht spurlos an ihren Haaren und Kleidern vorbeigegangen sein – gehen wir so los? Sitzen wir so an einer Bar? Oder gehen wir zuerst zu ihr, wo sie sich duscht, und ziehen dann weiter? So oder so ein seltsames Treffen mit einem fremden Menschen. Oder trinken wir ein Bier, wo sie arbeitet, wo sie jeder kennt? Lädt sie sich wohl immer Männer ein, die sie abholen sollen? Was denken die anderen Mitarbeiter wohl, wenn sie mich sehen? Ah wieder einer? Ich antworte, dass ich später vorbeischauen werde.

Ich verbringe einige Zeit mit Erledigungen aller Art und frage sie anschließend, ob es denn aktuell passe. *Ja klar! Komm einfach vorbei!* Also mache ich mich auf den Weg. Mit dem Fahrrad, denn es ist schönes Wetter. Noch während ich unterwegs bin, summt mein Handy und ich lese schockiert ihre Nachricht: Ich solle mir doch lieber jemanden mitbringen, da sie doch nicht so viel Zeit zum Quatschen habe. Wo soll ich denn jetzt jemanden herbekommen? Also sage ich ihr, dass ich dann doch lieber später am Abend kommen werde. Und so genieße ich eine spontane Fahrradfahrt durch das sommerliche Berlin. Die Abendsonne strahlt durch die Häuserschluchten. Ich mache mir meine Gedanken, suche mir ein nettes Plätzchen am Kanal, genieße den Sonnenuntergang, fahre zurück nach Neukölln, hole mir beim Türken ein Sandwich und falle zu Hause völlig entkräftet auf die Couch. Da summt mein Handy und sie schreibt: *Ach komm doch einfach vorbei.* Ich überlege kurz. *Na gut,* antworte ich. So eine Chance bekomme ich nie wieder. Anscheinend will sie mich wirklich sehen. Dieses Mal nehme ich die S-Bahn. Schon verrückt, wie voll der Zug an einem Sonntagabend so ist. Die Leute sehen ziemlich kaputt aus, denke ich mir. Viele davon. Ich bin entspannt.

Da schreibt sie wieder: *Vielleicht treffen wir uns doch lieber am Mittwoch. Da ist es entspannter.* Ich denke kurz nach. Da ich in diesem Moment am Ziel angekommen bin, schreibe ich: *Ich bin eben in Friedrichshain angekommen. Jetzt schaue ich auch kurz vorbei. Dann können wir uns gegenseitig begutachten und dann immer noch entscheiden, ob wir uns am Mittwoch nochmals in Ruhe treffen.*

Um auf das Areal zu kommen, wo sie arbeitet, muss ich zwei Euro Eintritt bezahlen. Das mache ich, trete ein und erblicke sie sofort. Natürlich sieht sie etwas anders aus als auf den Bildern. Das ist meistens so. Ich glaube, ich sehe aus wie auf den Bildern.

Sie blickt in meine Richtung, doch erkennt mich nicht, dreht sich um, schaut mich nochmals an. Jetzt erkennt sie mich, erstrahlt über ihr Gesicht und breitet zur Begrüßung ihre Arme aus. Mir bietet sich ein atemberaubend skurril schönes Bild: Da steht sie nun, attraktiv, lächelnd, mit ausgebreiteten Armen und bekleidet mit einer langen schwarzen Gummischürze, die über und über mit triefendem Fett, Sülze oder BBQ-Soße beschmutzt ist. Worum es sich genau handelt, weiß ich nicht. Vermutlich ist es eine Mischung aus allen drei Dingen. Vielleicht wirke ich irritiert, denn jetzt schaut sie an sich herab und meint, dass sie mich wohl nicht umarmen könne, so wie sie ausschaue. Ich antworte ihr, dass das schon okay sei und belasse es bei einem einfachen Hallo.

Wir unterhalten uns ganz kurz. *Ich muss nur noch kurz aufräumen und dann können wir los.* Da dreht sich wohl ihr Chef um und schnauzt sie leise, aber in einer nicht zu überhörenden Lautstärke von der Seite an: *Also, ich brauche dich hier noch mindestens zwei Stunden, das ist dir schon klar, oder?* Daraufhin dreht sie sich zu mir, lächelt, gibt mir einen Teller voller Rippchen und erklärt mir, dass es heute leider doch nichts mehr wird, dass ich aber gerne diese Rippchen haben könne. Ich bin begeistert, Rippchen for free. Ich lasse mir meine Enttäuschung nicht anmerken, sondern bedanke mich herzlich, genieße das Gebratene und verabschiede mich bald darauf von meinem Date. Leider habe ich diese tolle Frau nie wieder gesehen.

English version on page: 292.

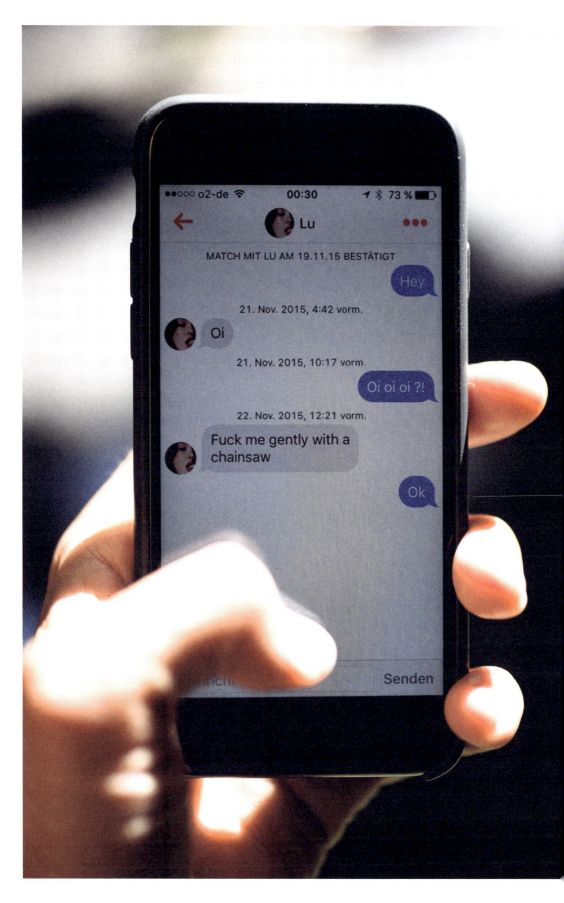

*Ich werde nie
wieder 25 sein.*

*Ich werde nie
wieder 30 sein.*

―――――――

*I will never
be 25 again.*

*I will never
be 30 again.*

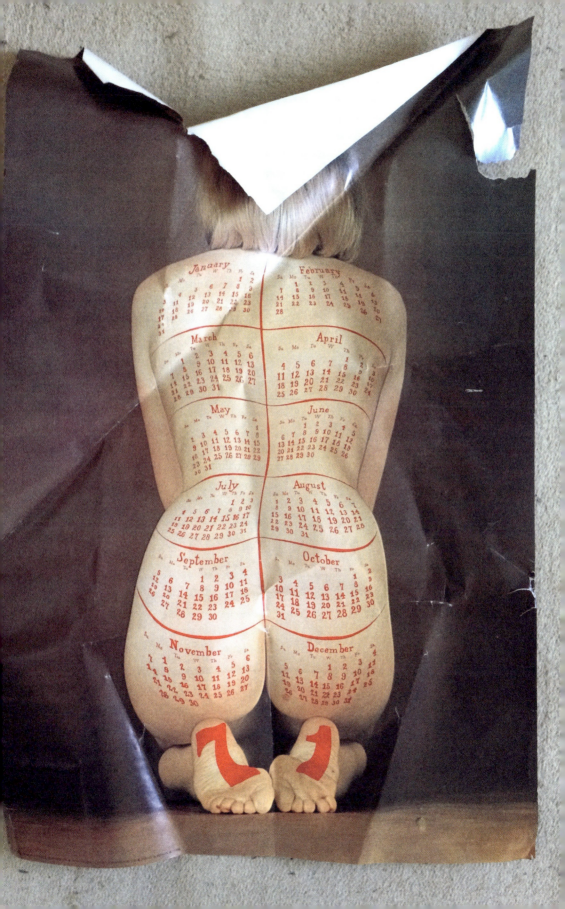

Was machst du eigentlich
die ganze Zeit?

————

What do you do
all the time?

Infos zu: 111 Project Leben

111 Project Leben — 97,67 GB
Geändert: Donnerstag, 26. Oktober 2017 um 22:22

Tags …

▼ Allgemein:
    Art: Ordner
    Größe: 97.666.984.191 Byte (98,14 GB auf dem Volume) für 3.646 Objekte
    Ort: Elements 1
    Erstellt: Montag, 6. Januar 2014 um 21:30
    Geändert: Donnerstag, 26. Oktober 2017 um 22:22

☐ Geteilter Ordner
☐ Geschützt

▼ Weitere Informationen:
    Zul. geöffnet: Heute um 17:47

▼ Name & Suffix:
111 Project Leben

☐ Suffix ausblenden

▶ Kommentare:

▼ Vorschau:

▼ Teilen & Zugriffsrechte:
Du kannst lesen und schreiben

Nur das Tun
lässt Träume wahr
werden.

———————

Only taking
action makes dreams
come true.

Stop thinking.

Start doing.

Zögere nicht,
um Hilfe zu bitten.

Don`t hesitate to
ask for help.

Höhenflug

Altitude flight

Erfolg ist eine
Frage
der Definition.

Success is a
matter
of definition.

Sometimes,
artists have to do shit
to survive.

Ein Kompliment.

Ein Sexspielzeug
für die Seele.

———

A compliment.

A sex toy
for the soul.

Es gibt immer wieder Momente, die mich unendlich faszinieren, aber für die ich gleichzeitig keine Worte finde. Hier steht ein Musiker unter einer betonschweren Autobahnbrücke. Ein riesiger Kontrast in einem farblich fast monochromen Bild. Er steht dort und spielt mit einem Instrument, verstärkt es mit einem Lautsprecher. Das Bild zeigt die Absurdität vieler Momente, gewährt Einblicke in menschliche Denkweisen. Doch es gibt keine Antworten auf ein mögliches Warum, sondern stellt höchstens weiter Fragen. Wieso hat er diesen Ort ausgewählt? Nur 50 Meter weiter wäre ein Park direkt am Wasser gewesen. Warum ging er nicht dort hin? Vielleicht erzeugt die dicke Betondecke über ihm einen besonderen Klang? Die Antwort kennt, wenn überhaupt, wohl nur er.

―――――

Time and again, there are moments that albeit fascinating me immensely I lack the words to describe. In this picture a musician can be seen standing under a heavy highway bridge made of concrete. He poses a huge contrast in an otherwise almost monochrome picture. He is standing there and playing his instrument amplified by a speaker. The picture illustrates the absurdity of any given moment but at the same time grants insights into the human way of thinking. The picture offers no clues as to the why; instead, it might raise even more questions. Why did he choose this place? Just 50 meters away there was a park right next to the waterfront. Why didn't he go there? Maybe the solid concrete ceiling generates a particular sound? Only he, if at all, knows the answer.

Unterhaltungen in einem New Yorker AirBnB:

Sie: *I am working tomorrow.*
Ich: *Where do you work?*
Sie: *In a strip club!*
Ich: *Ah – OK. What do you do there?*
Sie: *Oh, I am a dancer.*

In diesem Moment kommt ein Mädchen mit einer frisch geschorenen Glatze zur Türe herein. Sie erzählt, dass sie dafür 27 Dollar bezahlt habe. Sie findet, das sei viel. Da schaltet sich eine New Yorkerin in das Gespräch ein und fragt nach:

You paid 27 bucks to get your head shaved? And you think that's expensive?
Das Mädchen mit Glatze antwortet verunsichert: *Uh – Yes?!*
Darauf die New Yorkerin: *Oh no, that's not expensive, that's cheap.*
Das Mädchen mit der Glatze verwundert: *Yes? You think so?*
Die New Yorkerin voller Überzeugung: *Yeah! That's cheap! You know, it's very expensive to get your hair done in NYC.*

Conversations in an AirBnB in New York:

She: *I am working tomorrow.*
I: *Where do you work?*
She: *In a strip club!*
I: *Ah – OK. What do you do there?*
She: *Oh, I am a dancer.*

At that moment, a girl with a freshly shaven head enters the room. She states that she paid $27 for this and that she considers that to be a lot. A girl from New York joins in on the conversation and asks:

You paid 27 bucks to get your head shaved? And you think that's expensive?
The bald girl seems a bit shaken: *Uh – Yes?!*
The New Yorker: *Oh no, that's not expensive, that's cheap.*
The bald girl puzzled: *Yes? You think so?*
The New Yorker with great conviction: *Yeah! That's cheap! You know, it's very expensive to get your hair done in NYC.*

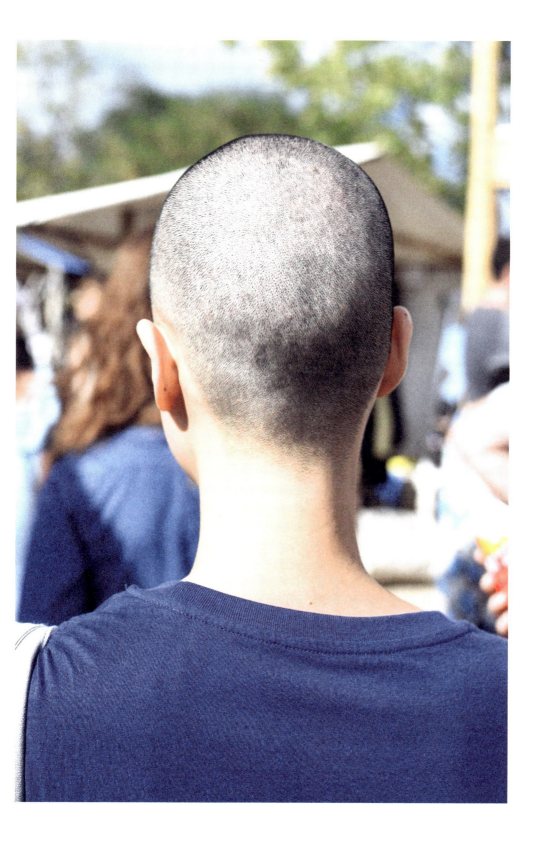

Hongkong

Berlin

Ein digitales
Portrait eines blinden
alten Mannes.

A digital
portrait of a blind
old man.

Erst 20 Jahre nachdem
die Menschen auf den Mond geflogen sind,
kam einer von ihnen auf die Idee,
zwei Rollen an einen Koffer zu bauen.

It wasn't until 20 years
after humans flew to the moon, that one
came up with the idea of putting two
wheels on a suitcase.

Fehlt
dir
etwas?

———

Are you
missing
something?

Vergiss deine Angst.

Ein stilles Lächeln
kann der Beginn der Liebe
deines Lebens sein.

———

Forget fear.

A faint smile
can be the beginning of
the love of your life.

Eine Bar voller Probleme.
Sie kommen mit ihren Problemen,
sie lassen sie hier.

———

A bar filled with problems.
They bring their problems with them,
then leave them here.

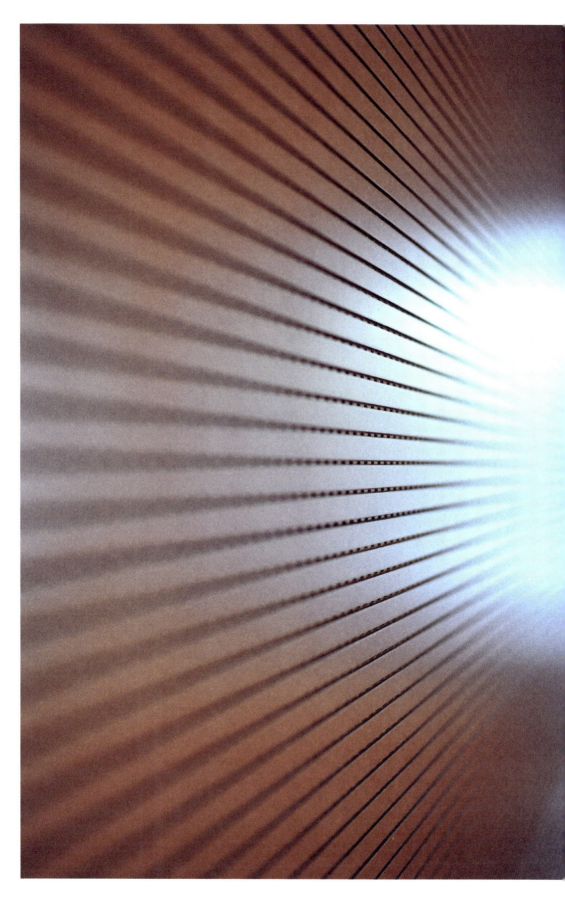

Ob die Hunde, die in den Gassen von Delhi
geboren wurden, wohl eine Ahnung haben,
dass sich außerhalb dieses Molochs,
die schöne Natur befindet?

———

Do the dogs that were born on the streets
of Delhi have any idea that outside of
this urban Moloch there's
beautiful nature?

In Paris betrinkt sich niemand. Der Wein liegt still
in seinem Glas. Alkohol ist zu teuer. Das Betrunkensein kann sich
keiner leisten. Dafür sitzen sie stundenlang vor ihrem Glas und
sinnieren und da sie bei vollen Sinnen sind, kommt dabei
vermutlich mehr heraus, als wenn sie betrunken wären.

―――――

No one gets drunk in Paris. The wine rests in its glass.
Alcohol is too expensive. Nobody can afford to be inebriated.
Instead, they sit in front of their glasses for hours pondering
life, and, since they are clear-headed, their output
is presumably better than if they were drunk.

Ohne zu leben, starb er.
Er lebte, bis er starb.

───────

He died without having lived.
He lived until he died.

Der Regen plätschert auf die Blätter nieder. Ich sitze in meinem Zimmer, schaue hinaus. Ich genieße es. Erinnerungen an vergangene Zeiten werden wach. Es ist meditativ. In seiner Tragik schön.

Rain is noisily falling on leaves. I'm sitting in my room. I'm looking out of the window. I'm enjoying it. I remember past times. It is a contemplative moment. Tragic, yet beautiful.

Wenn jemand jemanden hat,
nachdem zuvor beide einander hatten,
ist es für den anderen nie einfach.

―――――

If somebody has someone,
when before they had each other, it's
never easy for the other one.

Ein Mädchen auf der Straße zu
ihrer Freundin: *Weißt du, manchmal
würde ich am liebsten zu ihm sagen:
Du bist blöd, geh weg.
Aber so leicht ist das halt nicht.*

A girl on the street to her friend:
*You know, sometimes,
I just want to tell him:
You are stupid, go away. But it's just
not that easy.*

In Indien gibt es Geister –
weil die Menschen an sie glauben.

―――――――

In India there are ghosts –
because people believe in them.

Immer am Nachmittag, wenn die Sonne scheint, leuchtet meine Tapete in einem zarten Rosé. Es ist der rote Putz vom Haus gegenüber, der die Sonnenstrahlen reflektiert und dieses subtile Farbenspiel verursacht.

In the afternoon, when the sun is shining, my wallpaper glows in a delicate rosé. This subtle play of colors is created when the red plaster of the house across the road reflects the sunlight.

Die Kunst,
mit Nichts zufrieden
zu sein.

———

The art
of being content
with nothing.

Hoffentlich bin ich nicht einer dieser Menschen, über den andere heimlich lachen. Na gut, dann hätte ich wenigstens für ihre Belustigung gesorgt. Eine gute Tat.

Hopefully I am not one of those people that others are laughing at behind their backs. Ah well, at least I would have contributed to their amusement. A good deed.

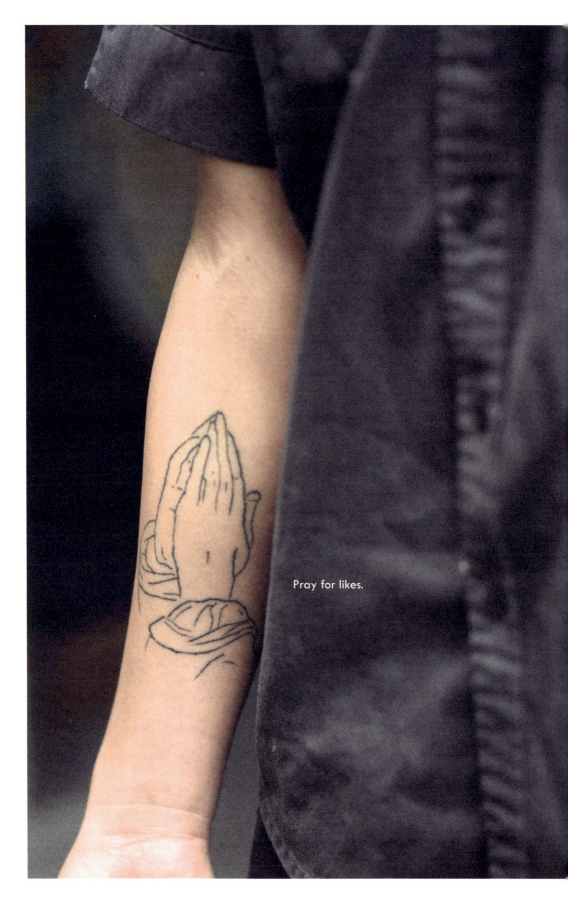

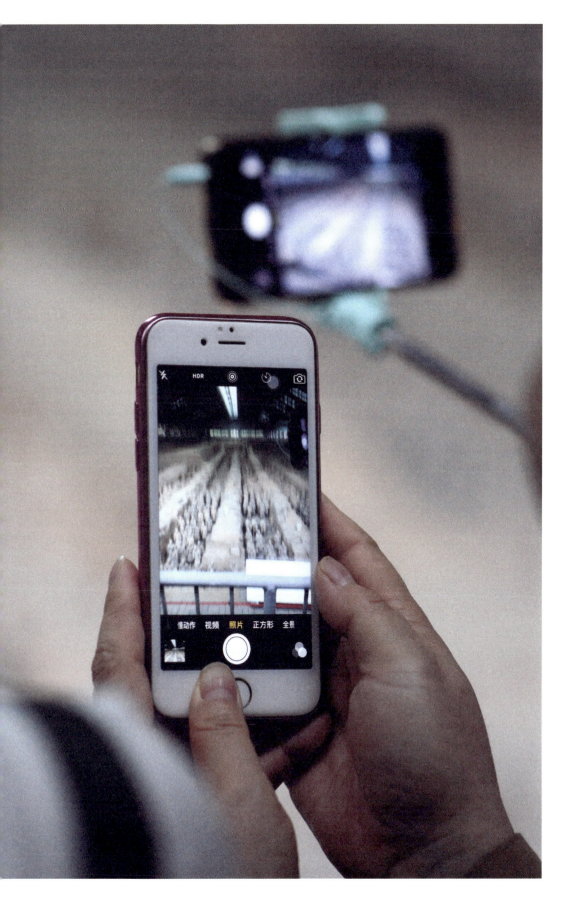

Wir versuchen immer
unsere Zukunft zu planen.
Doch wir verstehen
unser Leben
nur rückblickend.

We always try to plan
our future.
But it's only with hindsight
that we can understand
our life.

Schließe nicht die Türe
deiner Vorstellungskraft.

Denke in
Möglichkeiten.
Nicht in
Unmöglichkeiten.

―――――――

Don't close the door on
your imagination.

Think in
possibilities.
Don't think
in impossibilities.

SERENDIPITY

Von der Kunst, die Dinge
zu finden,
ohne danach zu suchen.

SERENDIPITY

The art of finding things
without
looking for them.

Hörst du den Wind in den Blättern der Bäume rauschen?

… oder einfach nur mal Nichts?

Can you hear the leaves of the trees rustling in the wind?

… or, just for once, no sound at all?

Sind dir schon mal die Augen eines einsamen Fremden aufgefallen? Im Nachtbus um vier: Ich sehe traurige Augen, Sehnsüchte, Wünsche, Verzweiflung. Alle sind auf der Suche. Nach irgendetwas. Nur wenige wissen wonach. Viele wissen gar nicht, dass sie suchen.

Gestrandete suchen nach Glück oder sind gestrandet vom Unglück.

Wir, in dieser Stadt, wohnen so dicht aufeinander, wissen alles über unseren Nachbar. Manchmal liegt unser Kopf nur wenige Zentimeter von seinem entfernt. Alles, was uns trennt, ist eine dünne Wand. Fast kann man sich atmen hören. Wir wissen, wann er aufsteht, wann er geht, wann er schläft, und hören mit wem. Aber trotzdem ist er uns völlig fremd. Ein Hallo im Hauseingang erschreckt und so kommunizieren wir über Zettel, anstatt an die Türe zu klopfen.

Die Stadt, Mikrokosmos des Lebens und manchmal Dystopie.

Have you ever noticed the eyes of a lonely stranger? In the night bus at four am: I see sad eyes, yearning, craving, despair. Everybody is looking for something. Only a few know what for. Many don't even know that they are searching for something.

Stranded people seek happiness or became stranded due to misfortune.

In this city, where we live on top of each other, we know everything about our neighbor. Sometimes your head rests only a few inches away from theirs. The only thing separating us is a thin wall. You can almost hear them breathe. We know at what time they get up, when they leave, when they sleep, and who with. Nevertheless, they remain complete strangers. A *hello* in the hallway is all it takes to scare us, and so we communicate via written notes instead of knocking on doors.

The city, a microcosm of life and sometimes a dystopia.

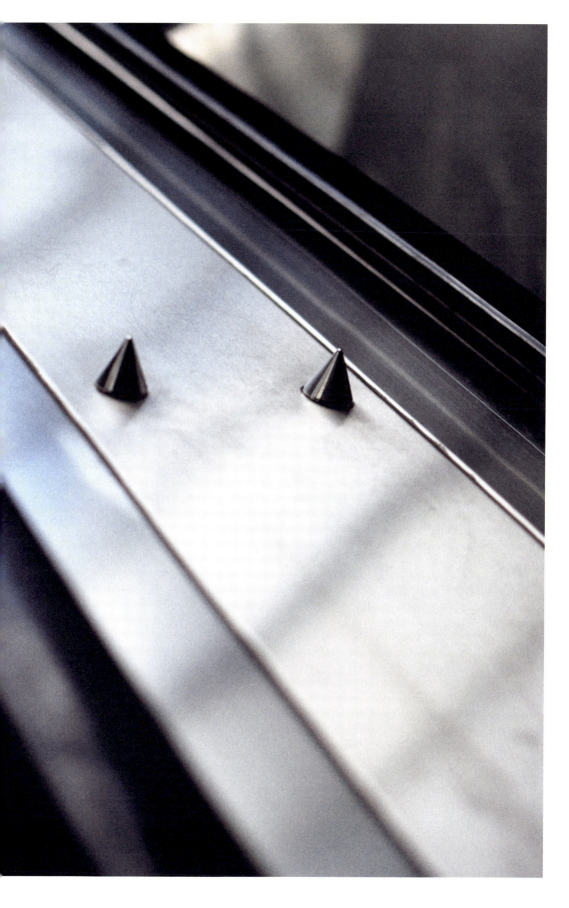

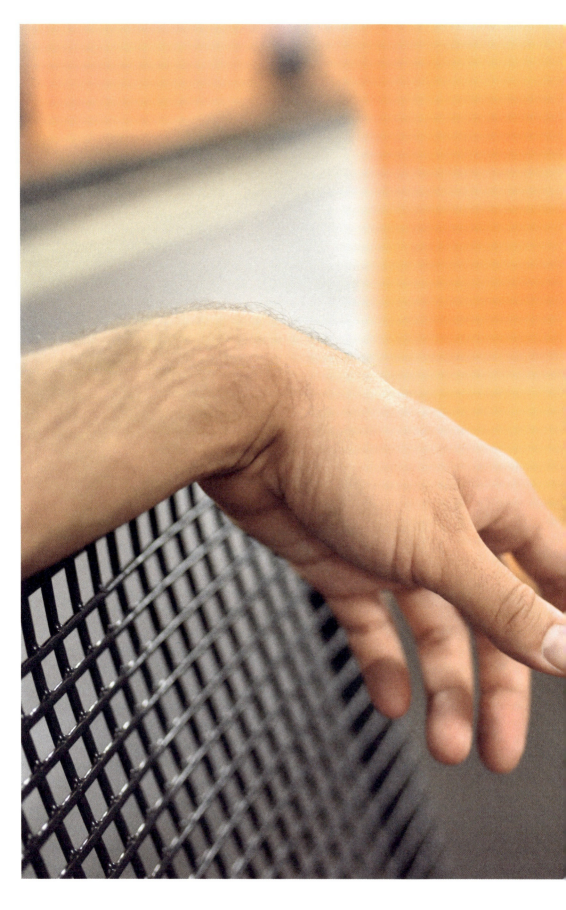

In NYC sind die
Mieten so hoch,
dass die Menschen
in winzigen Schachteln
schlafen müssen.

―――――

In NYC rents
are so high that
people have to sleep
in tiny boxes.

Ihr habt ne Rolex,
ich habe die Zeit.

You have a Rolex,
I have time.

Relax statt Rolex

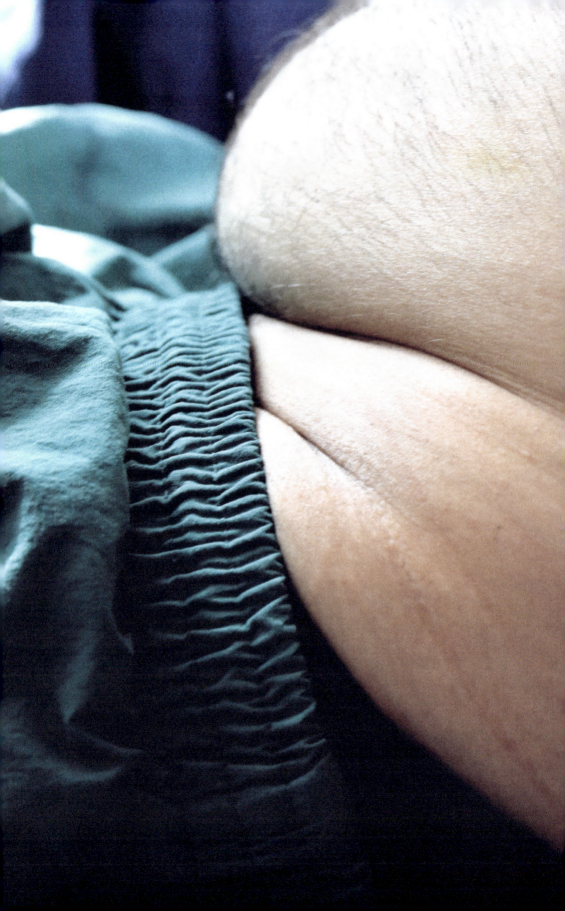

Ich sitze in einer mittelgroßen Stadt in China auf einem Stein und lese. Da kommt eine junge Chinesin mit ihrem vielleicht dreijährigen Kind daher. Sie spricht gutes Englisch. Nach einigen belanglosen Sätzen fragt sie, ob es möglich sei, ein Bild mit mir und ihrem Sohn zu machen. Selbstverständlich. Aber ihr Kind will lieber spielen. Es sträubt sich regelrecht. Sie packt es mit aller Gewalt. Es schreit. Es ist stark, fast stärker als sie. Die Mutter versucht trotzdem ein Selfie von uns zu machen. Doch ihr Kind wehrt sich mit aller Kraft, strampelt mit Händen und Füßen. Trotzdem gibt sie nicht auf. Unbeirrt versucht sie ein Bild von uns dreien zu machen. Doch ohne Erfolg. Manchmal bin ich auf dem Bild, manchmal sie, manchmal ein Fuß oder ein abgeschnittener Kopf, aber nie wirklich ihr Sohn und ich. Höchstens Teile von uns dreien. Irgendwann genügt ihr das. Sie bedankt sich freundlich und ich gehe, peinlich berührt. Einige Meter weiter spricht mich wieder eine junge Chinesin an, auch sie will ein Bild. Ich willige ein und sie ist überwältigt vor Freude. Ihre Freundin verdeutlicht mir, dass ich meinen Arm um sie legen soll. Die Umarmte kann ihr Glück kaum fassen, kichert wie ein kleines Mädchen.

Viele Erlebnisse vergleichbarer Art hatte ich auf Reisen in Asien. Ganze Reisegruppen standen Schlange, um sich mit mir zu fotografieren. Manche von ihnen, so hört man, hängen sich diese Bilder zuhause ins Wohnzimmer, stolz, einen Mann der westlichen Welt zu *kennen*.

Was macht dieses westliche Bild, das ich anscheinend verkörpere, so anziehend?

I'm reading while sitting on a stone in a medium-sized city in China when a young Chinese woman with her perhaps three-year-old child approaches me. Her English is good. After some trivial chitchat she asks if she might take a picture of me including herself and her son. Absolutely. But her child would rather play. He downright refuses. She grabs him with all her might. He screams. He is strong, almost stronger than her. Nonetheless, the mother keeps trying to take that selfie. But her child is fighting her with all he's got, hitting and kicking. Still, she does not give up. She is determined to get a picture of the three of us. Without success. Sometimes I am in the picture, sometimes she is, some shots feature a foot or a cut-off head but none of them her son and I. At best, you can see parts of the three of us. At some point she's happy with what she's got. She kindly thanks me and I leave, embarrassed. A few meters further along another young Chinese woman addresses me, she also wants to take a picture. I agree and she is overwhelmed with joy. Her friend makes it clear to me that I should put my arm around her shoulder. The one at the receiving end of my hug can hardly believe her luck and giggles like a little girl.

I have had many similar experiences while traveling in Asia. Entire travel groups queued up to take pictures with me. Some of them, rumor has it, hang these pictures in their living room, proud to *know* a man from the western world.

What makes this image of the western world, that I seem to embody, so appealing?

Ein neuer Kampf ums Bild
ist entbrannt.
Ein Kampf zwischen Bild
und dem Erleben.
Das Bild gewinnt. Wir verlieren
den Moment und die Erfahrung.

A new battle for the picture
has begun.
A battle between the picture
and the experience.
The picture wins. We lose
the moment and the experience.

A conversation in a posh eatery in Charlottenburg:
Are you going to the race this year?
Which race?
Well, in Monaco!
Oh, that one. No, I think we'll skip it this year.

Eine Unterhaltung in einer Charlottenburger Edelgastro:
Seid ihr eigentlich dieses Jahr beim Rennen?
Welches Rennen?
Na in Monaco!
Ach das. Nee, ich glaube dieses Jahr nicht.

Während wir von
selbstfahrenden Autos sprechen,
isst ein Großteil der Menschheit
mit Händen oder Stäbchen.

―――――

Whereas we talk about
self-driving cars, the majority
of mankind eat with their
hands or chopsticks.

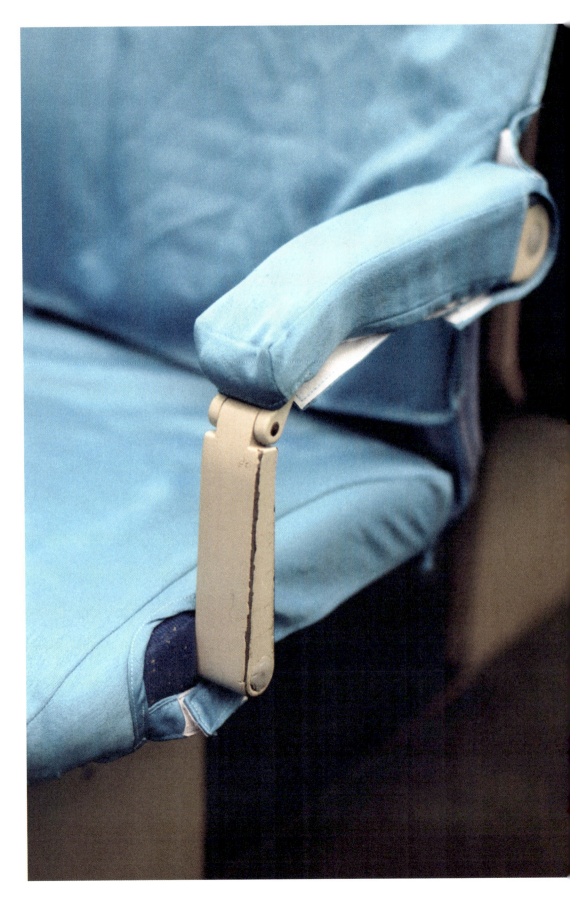

China

Who are the unnamed (Unbenannt) warriors in a digital world?

Ein Chaos hat auch immer
das Potential, dass etwas Großartiges
daraus entstehen kann.

―――――

Chaos always holds
the potential for something amazing
to emerge from it.

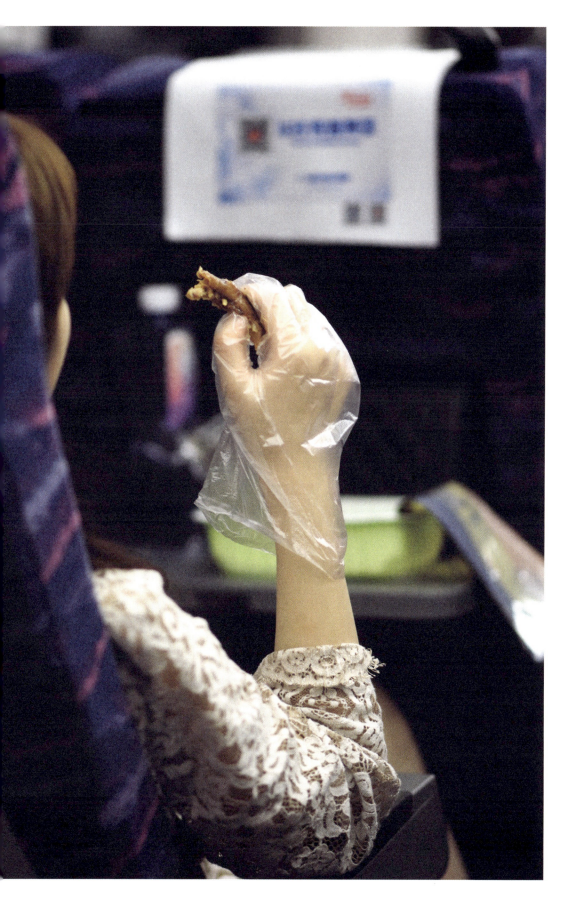

Es ist leicht zu kritisieren. Es ist leicht zu kopieren.
Aber etwas komplett Neues zu kreieren,
das es bis dahin noch nicht gab
und was noch niemand vor einem getan hat,
gehört mit zum Schwersten auf der Welt.

―――――

It is easy to criticize. It's easy to copy.
But to create something completely new,
something that so far didn't exist
and that nobody has ever done before,
is one of the hardest things in the world.

An den Titel kann ich mich nicht mehr erinnern

Ich sitze an einem freien Nachmittag zusammen mit Freunden und tue das Fatalste, das ich in dieser Situation tun könnte: Ich schaue auf mein Handy und checke meine Mails. *Ping.* Da ist sie. Die Mail, die ich nicht mehr erwartet hätte und mir nun für Tage meine Laune zerstört. Vor knapp einem Jahr hatte ich die Idee zu diesem Buch. Nun steht das Layout, die Bildauswahl ist final, alle Texte sind gesetzt und mehrsprachig lektoriert. Mein extern kommunizierter Redaktionsschluss war vor über vier Wochen. Fehlerquellen sind überprüft und überarbeitet. Eigentlich wollte ich schon vor Wochen in den Druck gehen. Eigentlich - denn es gibt mal wieder Verzögerungen, doch ich stehe in den Startlöchern und warte nur darauf, die Datei freizugeben. Und jetzt erreicht mich diese Mail von einem Galeristen aus Paris. Vor Monaten hatte ich ihn angeschrieben und um die Erlaubnis zum Abdruck einer Geschichte gebeten, die sich in seinen Räumlichkeiten zutrug. Doch in der besagten Mail verweigerte er mir seine Einwilligung. Hinweise auf ihn oder seine Galerie hatte ich bereits herausgenommen, doch er bat mich nun, von der Veröffentlichung der gesamten Geschichte abzusehen, mit dem Hinweis darauf, dass Unterhaltungen in seinen Räumlichkeiten Privatsache wären.

Zu diesem Zeitpunkt konnte es für mich kaum eine größere Frustration geben. Ich ärgerte mich nicht nur darüber, dass ich eine meiner liebsten Geschichten verloren hatte, sondern auch darüber, dass ich nun viele Teile des Buches neu überarbeiten musste. Ohne all zu große Anpassungen, konnte das vorhandene Layout nur gerettet werden, indem ich die Doppelseite behielt und mit einer anderen Geschichte füllte. Doch welche? Natürlich hatte ich noch Material in meinem Archiv, doch fühlte sich der simple Tausch der Geschichten irgendwie nicht richtig an. Die Idee, einfach die Seiten leer zu lassen, gefiel mir gut, doch ohne weitere Erklärung hätte dies wohl eher für Verwirrungen gesorgt.

Nun steht hier dieser Text über den Verlust einer Geschichte. Auf seine Weise gibt er Einblicke in etwas, das normalerweise im Verborgenen bleibt und zeigt die Herausforderungen und die Enttäuschung, die mitunter Teil einer (kreativen) Arbeit sind aber vielleicht auch einfach mit dazugehören.

Auf dem Bild links sind vier zusammengeschobene Buchstaben zu erkennen. Wer genau hinschaut, erkennt, aus den vier Buchstaben lässt sich das Wort NEIN bilden.

English version on page: 294.

Hast du dich jemals gefragt,
was sich hinter diesen berühmten
Gemälden von Warhol verbirgt?

Ein schwarzer Schatten.

———————

Have you ever asked yourself
what is behind those famous
Warhol paintings?

A black shadow.

Konstruiere
deine Zukunft.

Irgendwelche Ideen
oder Visionen?

———————

Built
your future.

Any ideas or
visions?

Zwei Menschen können
völlig unterschiedlicher Meinung sein
und trotzdem beide recht haben.

Das Problem ist lediglich, dass
wir zu häufig unsere
Meinungen für Tatsachen halten.

———

Two people can have
entirely different opinions and
at the same time can both be right.

The only problem is
that too often we mistake
our opinions for facts.

Vom Lebenssinn eines Lachses

Das Leben eines Lachses erscheint wie ein andauernder Kampf, voller Gefahren und Schmerzen. Von außen betrachtet, wirkt es fast sinnlos, doch gerade dadurch auch einzigartig faszinierend.

Ein Lachs wird in den Hochgebirgen Alaskas geboren. Frisch geschlüpft, macht er sich durch seine Instinkte getrieben auf eine lange Reise durch unzählige Bäche und Flüsse. Er ist noch klein, nur wenige Zentimeter groß. Sein Ziel sind die nährstoffreichen Ozeane. Doch auf seiner Reise begegnet er etlichen Gefahren, gerade als noch so kleiner Fisch. Trotzdem wandert er weiter, immer weiter, bis er sein Ziel erreicht hat. Dort angekommen, frisst er sich voll und so viel er kann. Einige Jahre verbringt er hier. Er frisst und wächst und frisst und wächst. Sein alleiniges Ziel ist es, so viel Fett wie möglich anzusetzen, um genügend Energie zu haben, um wieder zurückzuschwimmen. Zurück ins Hochgebirge, genau dahin, wo er herkam. Zurück in den Fluss, Bach oder Tümpel, wo er geboren wurde. Geleitet durch Intuition und seinen Instinkt findet er seinen Weg – unfassbar, über Tausende von Kilometer. Doch dieser Weg ist alles andere als einfach. Er kämpft regelrecht gegen Felsen, schwimmt reißende Bäche empor, gegen den Strom, bergauf. Er überwindet Stromschnellen und Klippen. Immer wieder wird er zurückgetrieben. Doch er gibt nicht auf, springt aus dem Wasser empor, schlägt auf einem Felsen auf und wird zurückgespült. Doch er gibt nicht auf, versucht es wieder, unzählige Male, wieder, wieder und immer wieder, bis er das Hindernis überwunden hat. Zwischendurch ruht er sich von seinen Strapazen aus. Doch auch das ist nicht ungefährlich. Bären wissen um das reichhaltige Mahl und lauern am Wegesrand, um nach den wandernden Lachsen zu fischen. Viele von ihnen fallen den Bären zum Opfer und ihre Reste düngen die Wälder Alaskas. Diejenigen, die es schaffen, wandern weiter, bis sie endlich die Gewässer ihrer Geburt erreicht haben. Dort angekommen sind sie sichtbar geschunden von ihrer Reise. Sie sind völlig abgemagert und übersät von Narben am ganzen Körper. Doch sie haben es geschafft und vollbringen ihre letzte, vielleicht einzige Aufgabe: Die Weibchen laichen ab, die Männchen befruchten die Eier. Direkt im Anschluss stirbt das Weibchen. Die Männchen bewachen noch eine Weile die Eier, bevor sie dann selbst sterben. Nach einigen Monaten schlüpft der Nachwuchs und der Kreislauf beginnt von Neuem.

Lebensglück
kann teuer sein.

———————

Happiness can be
expensive.

Happiness is our energy.

Ich sitze in einem Café und blättere in einer Tageszeitung von gestern. Ich mag es, in Cafés zu sitzen und in Tageszeitungen zu blättern. Nicht nur wegen des Zeitunglesens an sich, sondern um wunderbar unbemerkt die Gespräche von anderen Gästen zu belauschen.

Zwei jüngere Frauen sitzen am Tisch neben mir. Ich glaube, es sind befreundete Kolleginnen, Ärztinnen oder Krankenschwestern. Ihre Stimmung ist gut. Es wird gelacht.

… und dann, kurz bevor ich zur Mittagspause gehen will, stirbt mir der Patient weg. Wir dachten ja alle, der stirbt erst einen Tag später, aber nee (sie schlägt mit ihrer Hand auf den Tisch), *stirbt der noch vor der Mittagspause! Unfassbar!* Zwischenfrage der Freundin: *Welcher denn?* Na der Privatpatient, (mit einem Lächeln) *stirbt der einfach einen Tag zu früh!*

I'm sitting in a coffee shop leafing through yesterday's paper. I enjoy sitting in cafés and leafing through daily newspapers. Not just because I like reading the paper but also because it gives me an opportunity to eavesdrop on the other guests without getting noticed.

Two younger women are sitting at the table next to me. I think they are colleagues and friends, either doctors or nurses. They are in a good mood. They are laughing.

… and then, just as I was about to take my lunch break, the patient died. We all expected him to die the next day, but no (here she hits the table with her hand), *he just dies before my lunch break! Unbelievable!* The friend interrupts to ask: *Which patient?* Well, the private patient, (with a smile) *simply dies a day early, how dare he!*

Oft wissen wir gar nicht, was uns
wichtig ist oder was uns bewegt.
Unsere Gedanken sind wirr, aber
wir halten sie für klar.

Was ist dir wichtig?

_____

Quite often we do not know
what is important to us.
Our thoughts are wooly, but
we believe them to be clear.

What is important to you?

Ich sitze im Café *Les Deux Magots,* wo sich vor hundert Jahren die großen Künstler und Literaten der Zeit getroffen haben. Heute sitzen hier Einheimische neben Touristen und starren auf ihre Smartphones. Zwei Tische weiter sitzt ein Herr mit grauen Haaren und Dreitagebart. Er ist gut gekleidet und trägt teure, doch abgelaufene Schuhe, vermutlich aus Pferdeleder, zu erkennen an ihrem einzigartigen Glanz. Da kommt der Kellner mit einem Tablett zu ihm an den Tisch. Auf dem Tablett stehen eine Flasche Whiskey und zwei unterschiedlich große Gläser. Der Kellner nimmt das kleinere der beiden und bemisst damit die zu verköstigende Menge des feinen Getränks. Ganz genau bis zur Kante, ohne dass es überläuft. Anschließend kippt er es schwungvoll in das Größere, worauf er dieses vor den Herrn auf den Tisch stellt. Der Mann sagt ein paar Worte auf Französisch. Dann nimmt er das vor ihm stehende Glas und führt es mit zitternder Hand zu seinem Mund, nimmt einen kleinen Schluck und stellt das Glas, wieder mit zittriger Hand, auf seinen Tisch. Er kramt in seiner Tasche und holt ein ledernes Etui mit Zigarillos hervor, nimmt einen heraus und zündet ihn mit einem goldenen Feuerzeug an. Das Zittern seiner Hände ist nicht zu verbergen. Jede Geste strengt ihn sichtlich an. Er nimmt ein paar Züge, so zwei bis drei, dann wirft er den Zigarillo verärgert auf den Boden, kramt in seiner Tasche und holt abermals das lederne Zigarettenetui hervor. Er entnimmt einen und zündet ihn an. Diesen behält er im Mund. Er raucht ihn zu Ende, trinkt seinen Whiskey und schaut auf sein iPhone. Der Oberkellner oder Manager kommt herbei und gibt ihm die Hand, fragt, wie es ihm gehe. Er antwortet auf Französisch: *Sehr gut!* Nach ein paar Minuten winkt er den Kellner herbei, gibt ihm 20 Euro und sagt: *c´est bon.*

I am sitting in the café *Les Deux Magots,* where a hundred years ago the great artists and writers of that time came together. Today, locals sit next to tourists and stare at their smartphones. Two tables away there is a gentleman with gray hair and designer stubble. He is well-dressed and wearing expensive but worn-out shoes, probably made of horse leather, recognizable by its unique shine. The waiter approaches his table with a tray. On the tray are a bottle of whiskey and two glasses in different sizes. The waiter takes the smaller of the two and measures the quantity of the fine beverage to be consumed. He accurately fills it to the rim, without spilling anything. Then he pours the liquid into the bigger glass and places it on the table in front of the gentleman. The man says a few words in French. Then he takes the glass placed in front of him and with a trembling hand lifts it to his lips. He takes a small sip and puts the glass back on the table, again with an unsteady hand. He digs into his pocket and pulls out a leather case holding cigarillos. Takes one out and lights it with a golden lighter. The trembling of his hands cannot be concealed. Every gesture is a visible struggle. He takes a few puffs but then, seemingly annoyed, throws the cigarillo on the floor. He rummages in his pocket and again pulls out the leather case, takes out another cigarillo and lights it. This one he keeps in his mouth. He finishes smoking, drinks his whiskey and looks at his iPhone. The headwaiter or manager comes over and shakes his hand, asks how he is doing. He answers in French: *Very good!* A few minutes later he hails the waiter, hands him €20 and says: *c'est bon.*

Über Tausende von Jahren war es der
größte Traum der Menschheit, fliegen zu können.
Heute beschweren wir uns nur noch über
das Ölsardinendasein über den Wolken.

———

For millennia mankind's biggest dream
was to be able to fly. Nowadays,
when floating above the clouds all we do
is complain about being packed like sardines.

Ich liebe die Jahreszeiten. Wundervoll, dieser Moment, wenn nach viel zu langen, dunklen, grauen Nächten die ersten Sonnenstrahlen auf mein Gesicht fallen. Diese unendliche Energie, die wir alle plötzlich spüren. Die Freude, wenn das Leben um uns neu erwacht: die Bäume, die Vögel und unsere Laune. Irgendwann blüht es überall. Zunehmend werden die Tage länger – und die Röcke kürzer. Irgendwann ist die Luft auch abends noch herrlich warm. Es ist Hochsommer und das Abendlicht malerisch, die Sonnenuntergänge orange, blau und tiefrot. Doch die Tage sind heiß und anstrengend. Irgendwie bin ich dann auch wieder froh, wenn der erste etwas kühlere Tag daherkommt. Dann noch einer und noch einer. Ein neues Farbenspiel beginnt jetzt in den Bäumen: rot, braun, goldfarben. Einzelne Blätter segeln langsam zum Boden. Sie machen der Sonne Platz, die jetzt in einzigartiger Weise durch die noch vorhandenen Blätter schimmert. Doch dann, manchmal ganz plötzlich, schafft sie es nicht mehr, durch den dicken Nebel in der Luft. Aber es ist der Beginn einer wunderbar romantischen Zeit. Am liebsten bleiben wir jetzt zuhause, zünden uns Kerzen an und genießen diese heimliche Zeit. Alles wird ruhiger. Der erste Spaziergang in unberührter Schneelandschaft, wunderschön, eine eingeschneite Stadt, mitten in der Nacht, Schneeflocken wehen gegen den Laternenpfahl, in ihrem Lichtkegel beobachten wir, wie sie tanzend zum Erdboden fliegen. Irgendwann haben wir genug von diesem Winterspiel, die Kälte sitzt zu tief in unseren Knochen, der Schnee ist nicht mehr weiß, sondern schmutzig. Und dann, fast unerwartet sind sie da, die ersten Sonnenstrahlen und der Kreislauf beginnt von Neuem.

I love the seasons. It's such a wonderful moment when after way too many long dark and grey nights, the first rays of sunshine kiss my face. This infinite energy that we suddenly feel. The joy when our environment comes alive again: the trees, the birds and our mood. At some point everything is in bloom. Increasingly the days are getting longer – and the skirts shorter. Eventually, the air is still wonderfully warm in the evenings. It is midsummer and the evening light is picturesque, the sunset orange, blue and deep red. However, the days are hot and exhausting. I am sort of relieved when the first somewhat cooler day comes along. Then another one and another one. A new play of colors sets in and paints the trees red, brown, and golden. Leafs slowly start tumbling to the ground; they make room for the sun, which now gleams through the remaining foliage in a unique way. But at some point, occasionally rather suddenly, the sunlight no longer manages to penetrate the dense fog. Which, in return, marks the beginning of a wonderfully romantic time. We prefer staying home, light candles and enjoy this cozy time of year. Everything becomes calmer. The first walk in the unspoiled snow-covered countryside, beautiful; a snowed-in city in the middle of the night, snowflakes being blown against the lamppost, we watch their slow dance to the ground illuminated by the streetlight. At some point we are fed up with this winter game, the bone-chilling cold, the snow that is no longer white but dirty and grey. And then, almost unexpectedly, here they are, the first rays of sunshine and the cycle begins again.

Manchmal muss es auch
ein bisschen wehtun.

Das Gute besteht immer ein wenig aus
dem Schlechten und das Schlechte
hat immer etwas Gutes.

Ohne das Gegenteil wäre uns
das Gute oft nicht bewusst.

Sometimes it has to hurt
a little.

There's always
some good in the bad
and vice versa.

Without its opposite we often would
not appreciate the good.

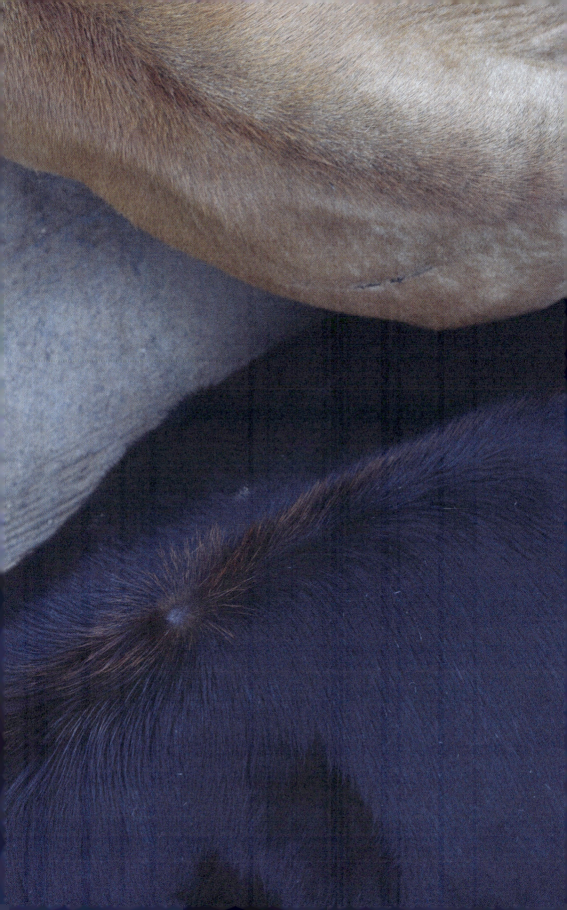

Schmusende Kühe.

Cuddling cows.

In einem Projektraum:

Fröhliches Mädchen: *Und? Wie findest du die Bilder?*
Ihr Begleiter, völlig irritiert, fast ein wenig schockiert:
Hä? Welche Bilder?
Jetzt ist sie irritiert, doch kaum schockiert, denn sie kennt ihn wohl. Darum antwortet sie fröhlich aufklärend: *Na da drüben, da hängen Bilder, das ist ne Ausstellung!*
Ihr Begleiter: *Ach so? Also, ich war an der Bar.*

———

In a project room:

A cheerful girl: *And? How do you like the pictures?*
Her companion, extremely irritated, almost a little shocked:
Huh? What pictures?
Now it's her turn to be irritated though she's hardly shocked because she knows him well. She happily explains: *Well, those over there, there are pictures, this is an exhibition!*
Her companion: *Really? Well, I was at the bar.*

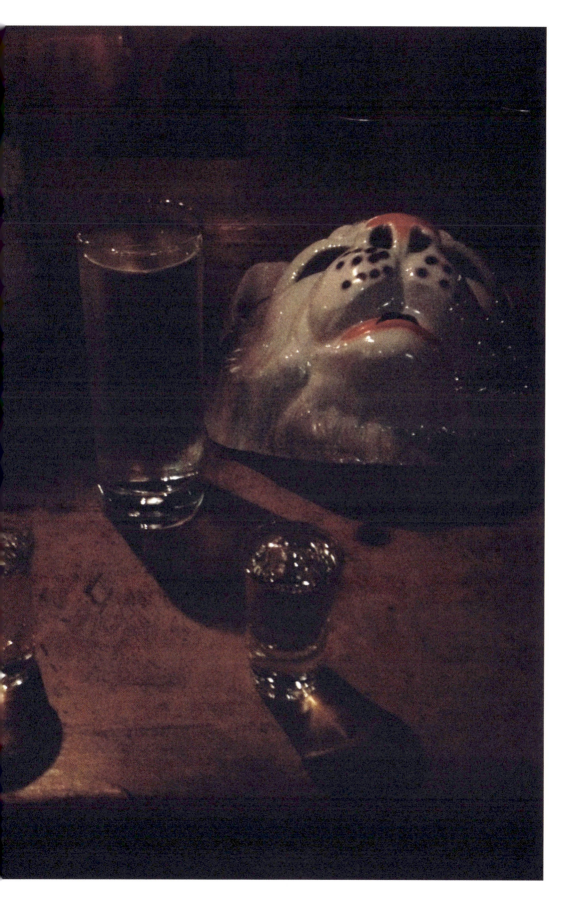

Sehe nicht die Probleme!
Suche nach Lösungen!

Don't look for problems!
Look for solutions!

Wenn du die Welt nicht verstehst,
konzentriere dich auf dein Umfeld
und gestalte deinen Mikrokosmos.

―――――――

If you don't understand the world,
concentrate on your environment
and shape your microcosm.

Kleiner Moment – du bist einfach großartig!

Eine Reise beginnt durch das nächtliche New York in einem alten roten Honda. Wir sind auf dem Weg über den East Side Highway nach Harlem. Ich betrachte die Skyline. Man sieht Bürogebäude und die *Million-Dollar-View*-Hochhäuser. Die Lichter brennen bereits – oder immer noch – in vielen Etagen und ich frage mich, warum. Es ist eine entspannte Fahrt. Ich träume und genieße es sehr. Ich bin mit einer jungen Frau unterwegs. Sie ist die Fahrerin des roten Honda-Flitzers. Auf der Rückbank liegt eine Bratpfanne. Ich frage, was es damit auf sich hat. Sie sagt, sie ziehe gerade um.

Wir besuchen eine Jazzbar in Harlem. Einer jener Läden, die ich gerne als ehrliche Läden bezeichne. Die Bar ist organisch gewachsen und nicht am Schreibtisch durchdacht. Ehrliche Läden erzählen meist eine Geschichte, oftmals aus einer anderen Zeit. Ehrliche Läden leben. Der Türsteher begrüßt uns mit einem freundlichen Lächeln und öffnet seine Türe für uns. Wir treten ein. Fast alle Plätze sind belegt. Wir werden zu einem kleinen Tisch in der Nähe der Bühne geführt. Es ist dunkel und die Getränkeauswahl überschaubar. Ich entscheide mich für einen klassischen Drink. Die Musik ist laut und unsere Unterhaltung zurückhaltend. Ich betrachte die anderen Gäste. Sie haben versucht, sich schick zu machen. Das sieht man. Alle schwarzen Herren tragen Hut. Auch drinnen. Ich trage ebenfalls einen Hut, auch ich behalte ihn auf. Ich beobachte die Musiker. Ihre Gesichter sind ein offenes Buch. Sie verraten alles. Der Schlagzeuger spielt ein Solo und sein Gesicht ist ein Zeugnis seiner Freude. Je schneller er wird, umso beeindruckender ist seine Mimik. Seine Augen sind geschlossen. In Trance gleitet er durch sein Spiel, wie wir durch die Nacht gleiten. Dabei behält der Mann am Klavier den Überblick. Er ist der Kopf der Band. Er sieht alles im Publikum. Schläft jemand, genießt jemand oder ist der Barkeeper zu laut mit seinen Eiswürfeln im Shaker? Er bekommt alles mit. Und reagiert darauf in der Weise, wie er spielt, oder mit einer Geste seines Körpers, einem kleinen Nicken oder dem Schütteln seines Kopfes. Und als die Musik verstummt, der Applaus geklatscht und die Drinks getrunken sind, sitzen wir wieder in ihrem roten Sportwagen und gleiten weiter durch die Nacht.

English version on page: 296.

Frei – sein.

―――――

Being – free.

Bisher sind es nur Gerüchte,
aber: Hipster sind die
gesellschaftliche Avantgarde.

———————

So far it's just a rumor but:
hipsters are
society's avant-garde.

A small note
on shit:

be aware:
shit happens.

Letztlich ist es besser
Glück zu haben,
als intelligent zu sein.

Ultimately,
it's better to be lucky
than smart.

Take your pleasure seriously.

Das größte Risiko
ist etwas nicht zu tun.

Denn meist bereuen
wir das später.

———

The biggest risk is
not to do something.

We're bound to
regret that later on.

Dafür
kann ich leben.

_____

I can
live for that.

Und wenn dir nicht gefällt,
was ich so mache …

… dann ist das auch okay.

And if you don't like
what I am doing …

… well, that's ok, too.

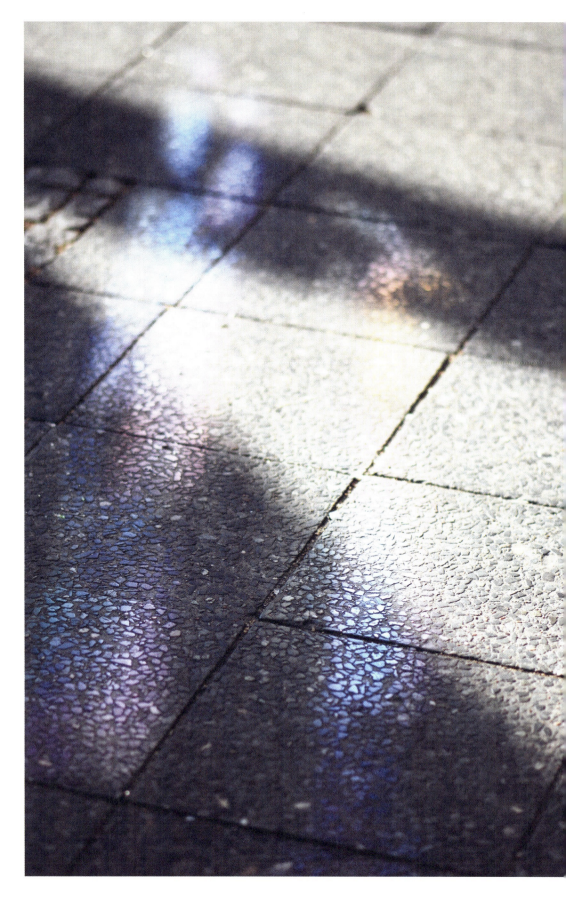

Die Gewissheiten von heute
sind die Irrtümer von morgen.

Und so bleibt die Frage
nach der Wahrheit.

Today's certainties
are tomorrow's mistakes.

Hence, the quest for
the truth goes on.

Worauf
wartest du?

What are you
waiting for?

Sei nicht so
ne Oktopussy.

———

Don't be such
an Octopussy.

Rise and Shine

Eine Blumenvase mit der Aufschrift: WE ARE GOING TO DIE. Sie lässt uns schmunzeln. Wir denken an die Blumen, die in ihr erstrahlen – doch nach und nach verwelken. Gleichzeitig trifft uns die provokante Aussage. Wir spüren eine gewisse Ablehnung, denn sie führt uns unsere eigene Endlichkeit vor Augen.

Doch der Schriftzug ist von einem Kreis umrundet. Als zweidimensionale Variante der Kugel ist er wiederzufinden in der Form der Sonne, des Mutterbauchs oder unserer Zeiteinteilung. Damit ist er ein Symbol für das Leben und die Zeit und bildet einen wichtigen Gegenpol zur Aufschrift.

Der Objekttitel lautet: *Rise and Shine*.

Wir alle tragen ungelebte Ideen mit uns herum, große Pläne, verschoben in die Zukunft. So bleiben es Träume in unbestimmter Ferne. Was hält uns zurück? Viel zu oft handeln wir nach vorgefertigten Denkmustern, werden zurückgehalten von oftmals ungerechtfertigten Ängsten. Aber – was wir zu oft verdrängen: Unser Leben ist einzigartig. Unsere Zeit ist begrenzt. Wir haben nur ein Leben. Daraus leitet sich die zentrale Aussage ab: Nutze die dir gegebene Zeit! Nicht irgendwann einmal. Nicht morgen. Heute! Jetzt!

Der Objekttitel *Rise and Shine* konkretisiert dies nochmals. WE ARE GOING TO DIE ist nicht nur ein Aufruf zum Leben. Es ist ein Aufruf zum Handeln.

A flower vase with the inscription: WE ARE GOING TO DIE. It makes us smile. We think about the flowers that are shining now but will soon start to wilt. At the same time, the provocative statement hits us. We experience some reluctance because it invokes our own mortality.

Yet, there's a circle drawn around the inscription. As the two-dimensional version of a ball shape it invokes the sun, the belly of a pregnant woman as well as our timekeeping devices. The circle represents life and time, and acts as an important counterbalance to the morbid inscription.

The title of the object is: *Rise and Shine*.

We all sit on unrealized ideas and are constantly putting off big plans. Thus, they remain distant dreams. What is holding us back? Far too often, our actions follow preconceived thinking patterns; unwarranted fears prevent us from taking action. But – there are things we push aside too often: our lives are unique. Our time is limited. We only have one life. Accordingly, the key message is: use the time you've got! Not someday. Not tomorrow. Today! Now!

The object title *Rise and Shine* seeks to substantiate this thought. WE ARE GOING TO DIE is not only a call to life. It is a call to action.

Erläuterungen, Gedanken und Nachweise

Umschlag: Weder die Kleidung, die Körperhaltung oder das Licht entsprechen einer typischen Schlafsituation, ein reizvoller Aspekt dieses Bildes. Gleichzeitig bildet die Denkerpose ein Gegenpol zum Titel, Berlin, 2018.

S. 4 Aus *I Like The Light*, es handelt sich um eine Fotografie, Berlin, 2018.
S. 6 Auf Wanderschaft in der indischen Kaschmir-Region im Himalaya, 2016.
S. 12 Ein kleines Pflänzchen, das sich wie durch ein Wunder im Überlauf unseres Waschbeckens ansiedelte, doch leider einen Tag später schon wieder leblos herabhing, aber mir dafür, weit über diesen Tag hinaus, sehr viel Freude bereitete, Berlin, 2017.
S. 15 Schachspieler am Union Square in New York City, 2016.
S. 17 Ein Flyer der Handsiebdruckerei Kreuzberg, erweitert zur Schlange, Berlin, 2016.
S. 18 / S.19 Spiegelung meiner Füße in einem Kunstwerk bei einer Ausstellung in Berlin, 2014. Das Zitat geht ursprünglich auf Edgar Allen Poe zurück: *Believe nothing you hear, and only one half that you see.*
S. 20 Überwachungskameras am West Bund, Shanghai, China, 2018.
S. 22 / S. 23 Neben den völlig unterschiedlichen Stilistiken ihrer Kleidung, die auf gewisse Weise typisch für die zwei Städte sind, halten beide Frauen ihr Handy fast identisch. Ein Verhaltensmuster, welches von vielen Menschen, unabhängig voneinander, aufgrund der Funktionsweise der Technik weltweit angenommen wird, Berlin / Shanghai, 2018.
S. 24 / S. 25 Zu sehen sind tatsächlich Hunde, aufgenommen im hohen Norden von Vietnam. Was ist nun richtig, was falsch? In China essen sie Hunde (oder eben auch im Norden von Vietnam), was auf uns schockierend wirkt, während wir Schweine zu Würstchen verarbeiten, was für Muslime eine Unart ist. Wir freuen uns über ein tolles Rindersteak, während die Tötung einer heiligen Kuh in Indien noch bis vor Kurzem mit dem Tode geahndet wurde. Richtig oder falsch? Normal oder abnormal ist oft nur, was wir aus unserer Sicht als normal betrachten. Entsprechend ist die Frage nach richtig oder falsch nicht eindeutig zu beantworten. Denn nicht die Chinesen haben seltsame Essgewohnheiten, sondern unsere Wahrnehmung macht diese Essgewohnheiten zu etwas Seltsamen. Ebenso kann ein Muslim nicht nachvollziehen, wie wir Schweine, aus seiner Sicht unreine Tiere, zu uns nehmen. Alles eine Frage der Perspektive und der gelernten Wahrheiten. Diese Erkenntnis kann auf viele Bereiche unseres Lebens übertragen werden, Vietnam, 2014.
S. 27 Zweimal *ONE WAY*, New York City, 2016.
S. 28 / S. 29 Zwei Beispiele für völlig unterschiedliche Denkweisen / Lebensweisen von Menschen, jeweils Berlin, 2018.
S. 30 / S. 31 Das Licht und sein Schatten bilden oft einzigartige Formen. Es ist ein Aufruf, diese zu schätzen und zu genießen. Gleichzeitig bestehen sie oft nur für kurze Zeit und sind damit auch Symbol für die Flüchtigkeit des Lebens. Foto: Ein wunderbares Lichtspiel in einer Galerie mit Deckenlicht, Berlin, 2018.
S. 32 / S. 33 Die Geschichte in der U-Bahn hat sich wörtlich so zugetragen und zeigt die einzigartige Weise, wie Kinder unsere Welt wahrnehmen. Das Erlebnis war für mich der Auslöser für die von mir von Zeit zu Zeit getätigte Aussage: *Ich möchte meine kindliche Naivität zurücklangen.* Das Auge stammt von der siebenjährigen Helene, Berlin, 2018.
S. 34 / S. 35 Hätte mir jemand die Aufgabe gegeben, einen Halbmond zu malen, ich bin

mir sicher, ich hätte gelacht, denn ich wäre davon überzeugt gewesen, diese Aufgabe mit Leichtigkeit lösen zu können. Denn schließlich kann jedes Kind einen Halbmond malen. In Südostasien schaue ich zum Himmel und sehe einen Halbmond. Er sieht anders aus, als erwartet. Er ist um neunzig Grad gedreht. Ein lachender Mund anstatt einer Sichel. Physikalisch einfach und nachvollziehbar zu erklären, erkenne ich wiederholt, wie verankert ich in meinen Vorstellungen über die Welt bin, und gleichzeitig: wie verkehrt diese manchmal sind. Die Erklärung, warum der Mond in diesem Teil der Erde anders ausschaut, als erwartet, leuchtet mir ein. Doch erst als ich den geneigten Halbmond sah, wurde mir bewusst, dass der Mond nicht unbedingt so ausschaut, wie ich es glaubte.
Unsere Vorstellungen sind durch unser Umfeld, in diesem Fall durch den Ort, an dem wir aufgewachsen sind, geprägt. An einem anderen Ort sieht die Welt anders aus. Andere Menschen sehen die Welt mit anderen Augen.
Wir denken in vorgefertigten Denkstrukturen, leben mit vorgefertigten Meinungen. Zu selten hinterfragen wir die Dinge, sondern glauben, was uns erzählt wird. Wir akzeptieren das Dargestellte als gegeben. Doch die Welt ist nicht immer so, wie wir sie sehen.
Es gab Zeiten, zu denen eine kleine Gruppe von Menschen davon überzeugt war, die Welt sei eine Kugel und keine Scheibe. Sie wurden als Irre abgetan. Ein kollektiver Irrglaube hatte sich gebildet. Aber solange die Mehrheit der Menschen glaubt, dass die Erde eine Scheibe ist, ist es schwierig sie vom Gegenteil zu überzeugen, Laos, 2014.
S. 36 / S. 37 Ein *Paradiesvogel,* der seine Papageien auf seinem Fahrrad durch Berlin spazieren fährt. Ist es nicht großartig, einfach sein eigenes Ding zu machen?! Sonnenallee, Berlin, 2018.
S. 38 / S. 39 Gleich und doch ganz anders. Dem Bild links hatte ich zuerst das Bild auf Seite 22 gegenübergestellt, doch dies benötigte ich für das Bilderpaar auf den Seiten 22 / 23. Ein paar Tage später stand beim UDK-Rundgang (Universität der Künste) die junge Frau auf Seite 38 vor mir. Ich überlegte nicht lange und fotografierte sie heimlich. Von da an sah ich fast täglich Menschen in Leoparden-Outfits. UDK Rundgang, Berlin, 2018 / Sonnenallee, Berlin, 2018.
S. 41 Es handelt sich natürlich um einen Ausschnitt des besagten Bildes, Berlin, 2018.
S. 42 / S. 43 Ein teures Auto, wichtig oder nicht? Zumindest für viele Menschen nach wie vor Statussymbol Nummer eins, Shanghai, 2018.
S. 45 Ein Blick von oben, bei einer Vernissage in Berlin, 2016.
S. 46 / S. 47 In Anlehnung an *Die Erschaffung Adams* von Michelangelo, Berlin, 2018.
S. 48 Aus meiner Serie *Supermodels*, Berlin, 2017 / 2018.
S. 51 Beachte die rechte Hand der Schaufensterpuppe, Secondhand-Store, Berlin, 2018.
S. 52 / S. 53 Schönheit und Vergänglichkeit. Links: Die Blume entwickelt eine wunderbare eigene Ästhetik, obwohl oder gerade weil sie vertrocknet ist. Demgegenüber die Suche nach und das Versprechen von Schönheit in unserer omnipräsenten Konsumwelt, jeweils Berlin, 2014 / 2018.
S. 54 Ein Kind liegt auf dem Boden und malt während einer Ausstellung, Berlin, 2015.
S. 57 Reizvoll, wie Gläser und ihre Schatten eine nahezu optische Täuschung ergeben. Wundervoll sind auch die Formen, die die Schatten der Tropfen an der Wand bilden, Ausstellungseröffnung, Berlin, 2016.
S. 58 Streetart von *Space Invader*, New York City, 2016. Copyright Artwork: Space Invader.
S. 60 / S. 61 Die Menschen, die in einer Stadt leben, sind dafür verantwortlich, wie wir eine Stadt wahrnehmen. Ohne ihre Menschen, ist sie nur ein lebloses Gebilde. Zum

Beispiel erscheint uns Kreuzberg als hip oder kreativ, weil dort spannende Menschen spannende Dinge tun. Noch vor wenigen Jahrzehnten war die Gegend als *Gefährdeter Bezirk* eingestuft, eine *No-go-Area*. Ziehen die kreativen Menschen irgendwann weg, wird ein Viertel oft langweilig. Doch wer sind die monetären Profiteure einer Stadt? Die Menschen, die in ihr leben oder andere? Fotos: Jeweils New York City, 2016.
S. 65 Altbaufassade, gespiegelt in einer Edelkarosse, Berlin, 2018.
S. 66 / S. 67 Die *Berlin Kidz* sind junge Graffiti-Künstler, die in wiedererkennbarem Stil die unzugänglichsten Orte der Stadt, wie beispielsweise Hochhäuser oder Kirchturmspitzen, besprühen. Hier ein Hochhaus am Kottbusser Tor, Berlin, 2018.
S. 68 / S. 69 Ein ehemaliger Schaukasten, ein verfallenes Paradies in Süditalien. Rechts: ein Stecker in Indien, Siracusa, 2018 / Indien, 2016.
S. 70 Ein Flugzeugflügel, über den Wolken, 2017.
S. 72 / S. 73 Ein Bahnhof in China, 2018, Straßenszene, Kottbusser Tor, Berlin, 2018.
S. 74 Ein schlafender Mann in Shanghai, vermutlich der Chauffeur, Shanghai, 2018.
S. 76 Die Platte *Love Life* der Gruppe *Berlin*, gekauft in Brooklyn für drei Dollar als Andenken an eine Reise nach NYC. Fotografiert zusammen mit meiner Plattensammlung bei mir zuhause, Berlin, 2018. Copyright Plattencover: 1984 The David Geffen Company.
S. 78 / S. 79 Es gibt keinen direkten Zusammenhang der Bilder. Es sind einfach zwei schön gestaltete Produkte, die zusammen wunderbar harmonieren. Links: Ein Aschenbecher in Paris. Es gab einmal eine Zeit, zu der Raummöbel ein so fantastisches Aussehen erhielten. Rechts: Auch die Rückseite eines Produktes kann für sich wunderschön sein, Paris, 2016 / Berlin, 2017.
S. 80 / S. 81 Das Bild thematisiert einerseits unsere permanente *Konnektivität*, spielt jedoch gleichzeitig auf die in unserer Zeit zunehmend einhergehende Vereinsamung an. Aufgenommen in einer U-Bahn in Shanghai, 2018.
S. 84 / S. 85 Links: Eine tatsächlich stattgefundene Unterhaltung auf Tinder. Rechts: Das Bild zeigt für mich die enge Zuneigung zweier Menschen, aber entgegengesetzt zu typisch vorherrschenden Rollenbildern. Die schwarze Frau scheint bei den beiden das starke Geschlecht zu sein. Er lehnt sich bei ihr an und sie hält ihren Arm fürsorglich über ihn. Jeweils Berlin, 2017 / 2018.
S. 86 / S. 87 Es ist schon ein paar Jährchen her, da saß ich mit zwei Freunden, die beide etwas älter sind als ich, am Tisch und wir philosophierten über das Leben. Es ging um die Frage, wann der richtige Moment ist, um das zu tun, was man schon lange tun wollte. Lieber zuerst Sicherheiten aufbauen oder besser die Unbeschwertheit nutzen, die einem jüngeren Alter typischerweise anhaftet? Es war eine Diskussion über Zeit und Geld und Lebensjahre und so weiter. Ein paar zentrale Sätze habe ich nie wieder vergessen: *Weist du, vielleicht habe ich heute Geld, aber schon morgen kann ich wieder arm sein. Und genauso kann ich, wenn ich arm bin, schon bald wieder zu Reichtum gelangen. Geld kann zu jeder Zeit da sein oder auch nicht. Aber diesen Moment gibt es nur ein einziges Mal. Jeder Moment ist einzigartig. Jede Zeit in unserem Leben ist einzigartig.* Und der andere Freund nickte und fügte hinzu, vielleicht sogar mit etwas wehmütiger Stimme: *I will never be 25 again. I will never be 30 again.*
Das fotografierte Kalenderblatt ist aus dem Jahre 1971, es ist abgegriffen, zerknittert, an manchen Stellen eingerissen. Ich fand es im Haus meiner Großeltern im Müll. Es ist in mehrerer Hinsicht Symbol der Zeit. Zum einen als Kalenderblatt, zum anderen durch die Spuren auf demselben und letztlich durch das Sujet der bemalten Frau, welches in

dieser Form heute nicht mehr zeitgemäß wäre, Berlin, 2017. Copyright Kalenderblatt: A/S Minerva Reproduktioner, Copenhagen 1970, Calender Girl – 71, Photo: Flemming Adelson.
S. 88 / S. 89 Nicht selten wird mir diese Frage gestellt. Manchmal auch als Aussage, in der Form *Du hast doch eh nichts zu tun*. Mich verwundert dies regelmäßig, denn ich würde mich als sehr beschäftigten Menschen beschreiben. Gleichzeitig ist es eigentlich eine Frage, die sich jeder selbst stellen sollte. Am besten immer wieder und wieder. Anfang 2014 begann ich meine persönliche Reise, kündigte meine konventionelle Anstellung und startete mein *Project Leben*. Zugegeben, manchmal weiß ich selbst nicht genau, was ich eigentlich tue. Aber langweilig wird es mir nie. So hat sich im Laufe der Zeit ein digitaler Ordner mit knapp 100 GB Datenmaterial angesammelt. Der Screenshot ist sozusagen die visuelle Darstellung meiner Produktivität, Screenshot, Berlin, 2018. Copyright Screendesign: Apple Inc.
S. 90 / S. 91 Work vs. Life. Bild links symbolisiert für mich die strikte, geordnete Arbeitswelt, Bild rechts hingegen eine freigeistige, individuelle Lebenseinstellung, jeweils Berlin, 2018.
S. 93 Mir gefällt die abstrakte Komponente des Bildes, die nicht verrät, was fotografiert wurde. Es ist ein goldener Lamettavorhang, von unten aufgenommen, Berlin, 2018.
S. 94 / S. 95 Am selben Tag, auf derselben Veranstaltung fotografiert, Berlin, 2018.
S. 96 Prothesen, die ultimative Hilfe, Berlin, 2018.
S. 98 / S. 99 Die Bar *Tiefpunkt* in Neukölln, vielleicht Symbol des Scheiterns vs. Bild eines Flugzeuges, Symbol von Freiheit, Fernweh, Exklusivität (historisch), Berlin, 2018.
S. 100 / S. 101 Meist verbinden wir mit Erfolg den beruflichen Erfolg (und damit einhergehend finanzielle Unabhängigkeiten). Aber was ist Erfolg? Im Allgemeinen, aber auch für jeden einzelnen? Muss Erfolg immer viel Geld bedeuten? Bedeutet Erfolg zu haben gleichzeitig auch glücklich zu sein? Man beachte die Frau unter dem Auto und stelle sich die Frage nach Erfolg noch einmal, Indien, 2012.
S. 102 / S. 103 Eine Fassade in Leipzig. Vermutlich wollte nur einer sein Eigentum sanieren, Leipzig, 2017.
S. 104 Merda d'artista (Artist's shit / Künstlerscheisse), May 1961, Aluminiumdose, bedrucktes Papier, 4,8 × ø 6 cm, © Fondazione Piero Manzoni, Milano, Foto: Privatsammlung, New York City, 2016.
S. 106 / S. 107 Ich treffe gestresste Freunde, gestresst von der Arbeit und mit Mangel an Zeit, aber dafür mit vielen plagenden Gedanken. Ich merkte: Was immer hilft, ist ein Kompliment. Ein Kompliment öffnet die Seele und verzaubert von Tragik verzerrte Gesichter in Freude über einen selbst. Schnell war für mich klar, ich wollte ein Kompliment kreieren: *And You Look Adorable*. Mit einem *And* zu Beginn als Verknüpfung zum Alltag und zu dem eben Geschehenen. Über Umwege kam die Idee des Stempels, denn damit hat jeder selbst die Möglichkeit, das Kompliment weiterzuverbreiten. Dazu eine Verpackung in Anlehnung an vergangene Zeiten, die viel weniger schnelllebig waren und einer Gebrauchsanweisung mit meinen Gedanken zur Idee. Es war mein allererstes Projekt. AND YOU LOOK ADORABLE, Berlin, 2014.
S. 108 Ein Mann musiziert unter einer Betonbrücke, Shanghai, 2018.
S. 110 / S. 111 Thema Freiheit: Links: Die Zimmerpflanzen sind drinnen eingesperrt, hinter einer Scheibe. Ihnen steht ein Pflänzchen gegenüber, das draußen vor der Scheibe, unter freiem Himmel, wächst. Rechts: Der Stacheldraht, Objekt von Grenzen, Absperrungen,

Ausgrenzungen. Ihm gegenüber steht im unscharfen Hintergrund des Bildes der blaue Himmel mit ein paar Wölkchen, Synonym von Freiheit, jeweils Berlin, 2018.
S. 113 Junge Frau mit ganz kurz geschorenen Haaren, Mauerpark, Berlin, 2018.
S. 114 / S. 115 BVG Bus Haltewunschanzeige STOP + cmd+C (Apple Tastenkombination für kopieren) = Stop Copying. Ein Aufruf: Kreiere dein eigenes Werk. Alles auf der Welt entspricht zunehmend einer Einheitsstilistik, inspiriert durch Instagram und Pinterest (Siehe ff Seite). Es ist doch langweilig, wenn es überall gleich ausschaut. Egal ob in New York City, Berlin oder Shanghai, überall dasselbe Bild, teilweise bis ins Detail, jeweils Berlin, 2018.
S. 116 / S. 117 Auf beiden Seiten praktisch das gleiche Bild: Medizinflasche als Vase, sternförmige Blume, silbernes Auto im Hintergrund, aber die Bilder wurden an zwei völlig unterschiedlichen Orten aufgenommen. Siehe oben, Hongkong, Berlin, 2018.
S. 118 / 119 Fotografie aus der Serie *Digital Portraits* mit dem Namen *Blind Old Man*. Ein älterer Herr sitzt in der Pariser U-Bahn, ein andersartiger, stilvoll mit einem lässig drapierten Schal, Ohrringen und einem individuell geflickten Hut. Wahrscheinlich ist sein Platz eher nicht in der Mitte der Gesellschaft. Er hält sein Handy in der Hand und verwendet eine Lupe, um das dargestellte auf dem Display zu lesen. Die Lupe ist ein Werkzeug aus der analogen Welt. Doch er nutzt sie, um die moderne Technik trotz seiner Einschränkungen bedienen zu können. Analoge und digitale Welt werden für ihn eins. Auch wir könnten uns fragen: Was ist unser Weg, mit der modernen Technik umzugehen? Doch das Bild ist nicht nur das eines Mannes in der U-Bahn, sondern es ist eine Fotografie eines Monitors, auf dem gerade das Bild mit dem Herrn in Photoshop bearbeitet wird. Auf der rechten Seite ist die Werkzeugpalette zu erkennen. Interessanterweise wurde bei der Programmierung auf die uns bekannte analoge Welt zurückgegriffen und die Werkzeuge wurden entsprechend benannt: ein Schraubenschlüssel, ein Stempel, ein Ordner.
Die Werkzeuge wurden benannt nach Dingen, die wir kannten. Die analoge Welt wurde digitalisiert. Heute verselbstständigt sich die Computerwelt zunehmend. Algorithmen erkennen Zusammenhänge und handeln eigenständig danach. Wir füttern die Programme nur noch mit unseren Daten. Viele der Programme werden nur noch einmal geschrieben und entwickeln sich dann selbstständig weiter. Aber wohin?
In der oberen Mitte des Bildes ist der *Hilfe-Button* zu sehen. Seit wir Computer haben, gibt es einen Hilfe-Knopf. Im eigentlichen Wortsinn etwas, das wir tun, wenn wir uns in Gefahr befinden. *Ich rufe um Hilfe!* Ich schaffe es nicht alleine. Der Computer, das Programm liegt außerhalb meiner Fähigkeiten. Doch dieser Knopf verschwindet zunehmend. Die künstliche Intelligenz tritt an seine Stelle und Hilfe können wir höchstens in den Tiefen eines chaotischen *Einstellungswirrwarrs* finden. Paris / Berlin, 2016 / 2017.
S. 120 / S. 121 Lichtverschmutzung, wir sehen die Sterne nicht mehr vor lauter Licht auf der Erde. Der rote Himmel ist das Abstrahllicht der Neonlichter, jeweils China, 2018.
S. 122 / S. 123 Stelle die Welt in Frage. Nichts muss so sein, wie es ist. Rollkoffer von oben am Flughafen Tegel, Berlin, 2018.
S. 124 / S. 125 Zumindest auf dem Bild fehlt etwas, vermutlich eine Statue, Berlin, 2018.
S. 126 / S. 127 Vergiss deine Angst, lächle und sag hallo. Inspiriert durch Anaïs Nins Worte: *Anxiety is love's greatest killer*, Berlin, 2016.
S. 128 / S. 129 Hate vs. Love. Haustüre in Neukölln, Vernissage in Kreuzberg, jeweils Berlin, 2018.
S. 130 / 131 Formen der Perversität. Beide Bilder habe ich unabhängig voneinander

gemacht. Jeweils war mir beim Fotografieren noch nicht klar, was darin zu erkennen sein könnte. Erst abends am Rechner beim Beschneiden und Drehen der Bilder kam dieses Paar zum Vorschein. Bei dem rechten Bild handelt es sich übrigens um alte Farbe, die von einer Hauswand blättert, jeweils Berlin Mitte, 2018.

S. 133 Eine typische Nacht in einer Bar, Berlin, 2013.

S. 134 / S. 135 Links: *Lichtexplosion* auf einer Wand, rechts: Licht und Schatten an meiner Zimmerdecke, jeweils Berlin, 2018.

S. 136 / S. 137 Es geht nicht nur um die Hunde von Delhi, sondern auch um unsere Denk- und Lebensweisen, in denen wir oftmals gefangen sind, Rotes Fort, Delhi, 2016.

S. 138 Paris, 2017.

S. 140 / S. 141 Die zwei Sätze beschreiben zwei gegensätzliche Arten zu leben. Foto: Metallgitter auf der Highline NYC. Die Kombination aus Licht und Metall erzeugt dieses einzigartige Farbenspiel, ein fast abstraktes Bild, New York City, 2016.

S. 142 / S. 143 Links: Ein *Streifenbild* entstanden durch Licht, Schatten, Heizungsrohre und Farbspiegelungen meiner Außenfassade. Ein Aufruf, auch kleine Details zu sehen, sich daran zu erfreuen und diese wertzuschätzen. Rechts: Das Taxi hat die Farbe meines Hauses. Gegenübergestellt aufgrund des ästhetischen Zusammenhangs der Bilder, jeweils Berlin, 2018.

S. 144 Regenszenerie, Macau, 2018.

S. 147 Ein Schachtdeckel, wie er in Berlin überall zu finden ist. Wir übergehen ihn täglich und übersehen das schreiende Gesicht, Berlin, 2018.

S. 148 / S. 149 Tragikszene in einer Kneipe. In eingeknickter Haltung sitzt das Mädchen alleine auf dem Boden, ein gefüllter Aschenbecher vor ihr, ihr Handy hat sie auf ihrem halbleeren Bierglas abgelegt und tippelt lustlos darauf herum. Nur wenige Fotos zeigen Traurigkeit oder Verzweiflung so eindeutig wie dieses, weswegen es trotz der schlechten Qualität zu einem meiner Lieblinge zählt, Kreuzberg, Berlin, 2016.

S. 150 / S. 151 Das Bild zeigt die Schönheit des Unschönen. Ein schönes Bild, obwohl der Reisebus alt und heruntergekommen ist. Zum Zitat: Was wir als wahr betrachten, hängt auch davon ab, was wir als wahr definieren oder woran wir glauben, Indien, 2016.

S. 152 / S. 153 Wir übersehen das Licht, dieses Wunder der Natur, viel zu häufig. Ein Hinweis, die kleinen Dinge im Leben zu schätzen und ein Aufruf, die Augen zu öffnen, Berlin, 2018.

S. 154 / S. 155 Ein Satz, der auf unterschiedliche Weise gelesen werden kann. Liegt die Kunst darin, kein Ergebnis als zufriedenstellend zu betrachten, oder darin, ohne Besitz zufrieden zu sein? Berlin, 2018.

S. 157 Eine junge Frau in China, 2018.

S. 158 / S. 159 Links: Tattoo eines ca. 18-jährigen chinesischen Jungen in Arbeitsmontur. Rechts: Sich überlagernde Kameras gerichtet auf die Terrakottakrieger in China. Die zwei Seiten thematisieren den alltäglichen Kampf ums Bild und das Streben nach Likes in den sozialen Medien, jeweils China, 2018.

S. 160 / S. 161 Viel zu viel Zeit verbringen wir damit, unsere Zukunft zu planen, anstatt im Jetzt zu leben, Flughafen Shanghai, 2018.

S. 162 Das Bild offenbart nicht sofort, was fotografiert wurde und spornt die Kreativität an. Es ist der Kern einer alten Matratze auf den Straßen von Berlin, 2018.

S. 164 / S. 165 *Serendipity*, meine erste *Konzeptuelle Fotografie*, mehr dazu unter www.felixsandberg.de/serendipity , erschienen als Edition, Berlin, 2016 / 2017.

S. 166 / S. 167 Städte gelten als effizient, das heißt möglichst viele Menschen leben auf engstem Raum. Aber wer fragt nach Sinnhaftigkeit? Nach Lebensqualität? Kann es bei einer Stadtplanung nur nach Effizienzkriterien gehen? Hongkong bei Nacht, eine der am dichtesten besiedelten Städte der Welt, Hongkong, 2018.
S. 169 Die spitzen Kegel zwischen zwei Rolltreppen, damit niemand den Zwischenraum als Rutschbahn verwendet, ein Symbol für eine *böse Stadt,* Berlin, 2018.
S. 170 / S. 171 Die Hand hat auf ihre Weise die fast gleiche Form wie die Berge. Auch die Farben des U-Bahnhofs und die des Sonnenuntergangs in den Bergen harmonieren, sind fast identisch. Trotzdem ist es ein Gegensatzpaar: Stadt vs. Natur, Berlin, 2018 / Himalaya, Indien, 2016.
S. 172 Ein Mural von *JR* in New York City, 2016, Copyright Artwork: JR.
S. 174 / S. 175 Wohnen auf engstem Raum. Dem gegenüber stehen die eingesperrten Fische vom *Goldfish Market,* die sich die Einheimischen gerne in ihre kleinen Wohnungen stellen. Eine schöne Analogie auf unser eigenes Dasein. Jeweils Hongkong, 2018.
S. 176 / S. 177 Die farblich wunderbar harmonierenden Bilder sind ein Gegensatzpaar. Die linke Seite zeigt die Magie der wunderschönen Natur, ein riesiger Wassertropfen *schwebt* auf einem Blatt. Dem gegenüber steht eine vereinsamende Stadt, mit Menschen in Hektik, mit ihrem Blick gerichtet auf ihr Handy. Die Farben beider Bilder sind ähnlich, aber in der Stadt sind sie von künstlichem Licht erzeugt, in der Natur sind sie authentisch, jeweils China, 2018.
S. 178 / S. 179 Zeit oder Statussymbole? Haben oder Sein? Eine Frage nach der Lebensauffassung, Graffiti in Neukölln, Berlin, 2017.
S. 180 Ja, das ist tatsächlich mein Bauch, jedoch bewusst unschön in Szene gesetzt. Heute bin ich natürlich deutlich trainierter, Berlin, 2018.
S. 182 / S. 183 Links: Der Blick aus meinem Fenster. Rechts: Die Überwachungskamera eines Berliner Unternehmers, gerichtet auf die Torstraße, jeweils Berlin, 2018.
S. 184 / S. 185 Die Bilder thematisieren Mobilität im Allgemeinen, eine autogerechte Stadt, und zeigen am Beispiel des unnötigen Energieverbrauchs absurde menschliche Denkweisen. Darüber hinaus harmonieren sie durch die gegenläufige *Kurve,* die in jedem der beiden Bilder auftaucht. Im rechten Bild faszinieren mich die fließenden Formen der Spiegelungen, die durch das harte Design des Kotflügels entstehen und an ein psychedelisches Bild erinnern, Shanghai, 2018 / Berlin, 2018.
S. 187 Die eigentliche *Attraktion* auf dem Bild ist aufgrund der Smartphones und Kameras nicht zu sehen. In dem Auto sitzt der Dalai Lama, Indien, 2016.
S. 188 / S. 189 Ein teuflisches Auto, Shanghai, 2018.
S. 190 Die wohl entlegenste Region, die ich je besuchte. Hoch oben im Himalaya, in einer Gegend, die nur zu Fuß erreichbar ist, war ich der zweite Mensch der westlichen Welt, den die Kinder eines Kaschmirbauers zu Gesicht bekommen haben. Zuerst waren sie äußerst schüchtern, doch dann entdeckten sie das Spiel mit meiner Kamera, zeigten mir ihre Ziegen, inszenierten sich mit ihnen und wollten immer wieder und wieder fotografiert werden, Indien, 2016.
S. 192 / S. 193 Technisches Versagen. Links: Transrapid in Shanghai. Das ehemalige technologische Flaggschiff ist in die Jahre gekommen, die Sitze abgewetzt, die Griffe abgerieben. Ein technologisches Konzept, was wegweisend war, aber sich durch unglückliche Zufälle nicht durchgesetzt hat. Rechts: Ein iPhone, Wegbereiter unseres heutigen Technologieumfeldes. Doch auch dieses ist nicht unfehlbar: Das Display ist

zersprungen, der Home-Button funktioniert nicht mehr und muss über die interne App gesteuert werden. Doch das Display leuchtet wunderbar golden durch das auf ihm dargestellte Bild, Shanghai, 2018 / Berlin, 2018.

S. 194 / S. 195 Der Algorithmus von iPhoto versucht den Gesichtern der Terrakottakrieger einen Namen zuzuordnen. Da er keine vergleichbare Person in meiner Datenbank findet, bezeichnet er sie als *Unbenannt*. Dass es sich nicht um Menschen handelt, erkennt die Software nicht. Ein Beispiel für das Nicht-Funktionieren mancher Algorithmen, Berlin, 2018. Screenshot aus iPhoto, Copyright iPhotomaske Apple Inc.

S. 196 / S. 197 Inspiriert durch *Nietzsches* Prolog in *Also sprach Zarathustra*: *Man muss noch Chaos in sich haben, um einen tanzenden Stern gebären zu können*, Berlin, 2019.

S. 198 / S. 199 Verpflegung unterwegs. Rechts: Ein Mädchen knabbert Hühnerfüße im Hochgeschwindigkeitszug. Sie trägt ganz leichte Plastikhandschuhe, die anschließend entsorgt werden. So spart sie sich das Händewaschen, Berlin, 2018 / China, 2018.

S. 200 / S. 201 Die Aussage bezieht sich auf scheinbar so einfache Dinge wie beispielsweise die Bilder von Jackson Pollock oder Arbeiten von Martin Creed. Foto: Eine völlig neuartige Skulptur eines Unbekannten, Berlin, 2018.

S. 202 Vier Buchstaben auf meinem Fensterbrett, die zusammen das Wort NEIN ergeben, Berlin, 2019.

S. 205 New York City, 2016.

S. 207 Baustelle des Axel Springer Neubaus, Berlin, 2018.

S. 208 / S. 209 Bei den meisten Statements handelt es sich um Meinungen und selten um Tatsachen. Trotzdem wird oft stundenlang über Meinungen, als wären es Tatsachen, diskutiert. *If we have data, let's look at data. If all we have are opinions, let's go with mine.* – Jim F. Barksdale. Foto: Himmel in Südostasien, 2015.

S. 210 / S. 211 Mich beeindruckt der Lachs. Er schindet sich einmal um die halbe Welt, um dann wieder zurückzuschwimmen. Ein Sinn ist nicht zu erkennen. Er lebt sein Leben einfach, getrieben von seinen Instinkten, Kanada, 2006.

S. 212 / S. 213 Glück ist omnipräsent in unserer heutigen Konsum- und Werbewelt. Kaufe und werde dadurch glücklich. Das Bild hingegen zeigt nur Leere, keine Wohnlichkeit, alles andere als ein glückliches Lebensumfeld. Dabei gilt für viele gerade das Eigenheim, zeitgemäß mit großen Fenstern, als besonders erstrebenswertes Lebensziel, Berlin, 2018.

S. 214 / S. 215 Erkenne die kleinen Freuden im Leben, wie beispielsweise eine Steckdose in Kopenhagen, 2017.

S. 216 *We deserve to be happy*, Berlin, 2018.

S. 218 / S. 219 *Little Black Box*. Eine Box für all deine Wünsche, Ideen, Träume oder aber für Dinge, die du hinter dir lassen willst. Wähle bewusst, denn wenn du die Schachtel einmal verschließt, lässt sie sich nicht wieder öffnen. Mehr dazu: www.felixsandberg.de/little-black-box , Berlin, 2016.

S. 221 Paris von oben, Paris, 2017.

S. 222 / S. 223 Ganz allgemein: Schätze die gefühlten Selbstverständlichkeiten, Ostsee, 2018.

S. 225 Ein vertrocknetes Blatt. Mich faszinieren die *Rillen* im Stiel, Siracusa, 2018.

S. 226 / S. 227 Ähnlich wie mit den Sonnenstrahlen nach einem kalten Winter (siehe Seite 224), verhält es sich auch mit der Freude über ein vollendetes Projekt. Ein großartiges Gefühl und es ist umso größer, je schwerer der Weg dahin war. Etwas zu kreieren, in welcher Form auch immer, ist niemals einfach. Die Entbehrungen, die Zeit, der Frust, das investierte Kapital, der Schweiß, viel ist notwendig, um ein Ziel zu erreichen. Gerade weil es schwierig ist, versucht oder schafft es eben nicht jeder. Genau darin liegt die Begründung, warum wir in Form eines *toll!*, *schön!*, *beeindruckend!* oder im Idealfall in Form eines Verkaufes Ansehen erlangen. Wäre es keine harte Arbeit, wäre es etwas Normales und würde damit weder von außen noch von uns selbst als etwas Besonderes wahrgenommen werden. Ein Kaktus auf meinem Fensterbrett. Auch er tut mir manchmal weh, doch gerade das macht ihn auch besonders, Berlin, 2016.

S. 228 Zwei Kühe eng aneinandergekuschelt, Indien, 2016.

S. 231 Eine Bar in Neukölln. Ich mag die surreale Komponente der Maske auf dem Tisch. Wie es wohl dazu kam? Berlin, 2014.

S. 233 Eine Mauer im Weg. Beispiel der Absurdität menschlicher Handlungen, Shanghai, 2018.

S. 235 Das Bild entstand in einem Linienbus in China. Der Fahrer, so trist seine Arbeit vermutlich an manchen Tagen ist, hatte vorne auf der Ablage, direkt neben den Türen, zwei kleine Zimmerpflanzen stehen, um die er sich offensichtlich kümmerte und die ihn und die Fahrgäste erfreuen, China, 2018.

S. 236 / S. 237 *Serendipity II*, Paris / Berlin, 2017.

S. 239 Ein weiteres Jazzkonzert auf dieser Reise, sehr experimentell und mit dem Sonnenuntergang im Hintergrund eines der schönsten Erlebnisse des Jahres, New York City, 2016.

S. 240 Macau, 2018.

S. 242 Trends sind heute so schnell, manchmal weiß man nicht, ob das, was man sich am Abend vorher rausgelegt hat, am Tag darauf noch *in* ist. Was Hipster heute tragen und worüber einige manchmal lachen, trägt die breite Masse oft nur wenige Zeit später. Nur haben viele von ihnen zu diesem Zeitpunkt schon wieder vergessen, dass sie einst darüber lachten, Kunsthochschule Weissensee, Berlin, 2018.

S. 245 Mural in New York City, Zitat und Bild entnommen aus *Moodboard New York City*, www.felixsandberg.de/moodboard-nyc , NYC, 2016.

S. 246 / S. 247 Shit happens, take it easy, Berlin, 2018 / New York City, 2016.

S. 248 / S. 249 Manchmal hat man es einfach nicht in der Hand. Oft entscheidet der Zufall über Erfolg und Misserfolg (was auch immer das ist). Man kann zu früh sein, zu spät oder eben im richtigen Moment am richtigen Ort. Wirklich beeinflussen kann man es nicht. Ein Freund von mir arbeitet bei einem großen Konsumgüterhersteller. Bei gleichen Ressourcen, Manpower, Agenturen und so weiter, funktioniert die eine Hälfte der Produkte und die andere funktioniert nicht und keiner weiß warum. Dieses Bild hätte ich wohl kaum planen können. Es ist ein Produkt des Zufalls, Berlin, 2016.

S. 250 / S. 251 Rechts: Ein älterer Herr, der mit seinem Akkordeon auf dem Tempelhofer Feld sitzt, spielt und in den Sonnenuntergang schaut. Wie wundervoll. Zitat: Charles Eames. Links: Ein Ledergerüst für besondere sexuelle Vorlieben. Was auch immer deine Freuden sind, nimm sie ernst, jeweils Berlin, 2018.

S. 252 Wohl spontan besprühte Matratze auf den Straßen von Neukölln, Berlin, 2017.

S. 254 / S. 255 Mein Streetart Projekt *Money Makes Me Happy*. Erst im Laufe der Zeit, wenn das Kupfer oxidiert, kommt der Smiley darauf zum Vorschein, Berlin, 2017.

S. 256 / S. 257 Es gibt kaum etwas auf der Welt, was alle Menschen gleich gut finden. Ein Nein heißt nicht notwendigerweise, dass die Qualität der Arbeit schlecht ist. Vielleicht trifft sie einfach nicht den Geschmack eben dieser Person, dafür aber vielleicht den von vielen anderen. Bei vielen Läden habe ich angefragt, ob sie meine Produkte führen wollen und oftmals auch ein Nein erhalten. Aber gleichzeitig gab und gibt es auch genügend, die von meinen Arbeiten begeistert waren und sind. Viele Blogs habe ich angeschrieben, die jedoch nichts über mich schreiben wollten, aber andere meldeten sich dafür ohne mein Zutun. Ein Nein ist Teil des (kreativen) Schaffens. Auch wenn dies mitunter frustriert, vertraue auf dich und arbeite an deinen Träumen, Berlin, 2018.

S. 258 / S. 259 Ich weiß nicht, was ich zu diesen Bildern schreiben soll, aber ich finde, sie sehen zusammen einfach wunderbar aus. Links: Spiegelungen auf der Straße. Ich weiß nicht, woher sie kamen, doch es waren eindeutig Spiegelungen. Alle Passanten um mich herum gingen unbemerkt an diesem wunderbaren Farbenspiel vorüber. Rechts: Alter Mercedes in Tegel, jeweils Berlin, 2018.

S. 260 Eines Abends ging ich mit Freunden durch die Straßen und entdeckte den Schatten eines kleinen Männchens an dem Toilettenhäuschen einer Baustelle. Ich war begeistert, meine Freunde lachten mich aus. Als ich einige Stunden später auf meinem Nachhauseweg wieder an der Baustelle vorbeiging, war der Schatten immer noch sichtbar. Es war mitten in der Nacht, ich holte meine Kamera, kehrte zurück und fotografierte das Männchen. Am nächsten Abend war es verschwunden. Das Bild ist das einzige Zeugnis einer inspirierenden Nacht. Was siehst du auf diesem Bild? Berlin, 2016.

S. 262 / S. 263 Die quälende Entscheidung, welche Socken ich anziehe, Berlin, 2017.

S. 265 Eine Wartehalle für den Bus in China, 2018.

S. 266 Die wunderbare Natur, die zufällig einzigartige Formen hervorbringt. Hier die eines Oktopus – zumindest ich sehe ihn, Berlin, 2016.

S. 268 - S. 271 *Rise and Shine*, mehr dazu: www.felixsandberg.de/rise-and-shine , Berlin, 2015.

S. 298 - S. 301 Eine Parodie auf die oft stark verklausulierten Beschreibungstexte bei Ausstellungen, Bild: Familienfoto, Süddeutschland 1988.

S. 303 Selbstportrait im Spiegel mit dem letzten Bild des Films, nachdem ich die Serie *Supermodels* fotografierte. Bewusst sind darauf Staubkörner und Kratzer zu sehen, denn das Bild wurde als Verweis auf die verwendete analoge Technik nicht vollständig retuschiert. Ich mag das Bild sehr, denn mir ist darauf die Anstrengung des Tages deutlich anzusehen, aber gleichzeitig auch eine tiefe Entspanntheit, begründet durch die Freude über das Geschaffte, Berlin, 2018.

Explanatory notes, thoughts and references

Cover: me on my bed. Neither the shirt, the posture nor the light depict a typical sleeping environment, which to me makes this picture particularly appealing. At the same time, the pose of a thinker forms a contrast to the title, Berlin, 2018.

p. 4 From *I Like The Light,* photo series, Berlin, 2018.
p. 6 Traveling in the Indian Kashmir region in the Himalayas, 2016.
p. 12 A small plant that miraculously colonized the overflow of our sink that, unfortunately, had already wilted by the next day but given me a lot of joy on this day (and beyond), Berlin, 2017.
p. 15 Chess players at Union Square in New York City, 2016.
p. 17 A drawing of a snake on a flyer of the *Handsiebdruckerei* Kreuzberg, Berlin, 2016.
p. 18 / p. 19 Reflection of my feet in a piece of art at an exhibition, Berlin, 2014. The quote is originally from Edgar Allen Poe: *Believe nothing you hear, and only one half that you see.*
p. 20 Surveillance cameras at the West Bund, Shanghai, China, 2018.
p. 22 / p. 23 Apart from the completely different styles of dress that in a way are representative of the two cities, both women are holding their cell phones in an almost identical manner. A new behavioral pattern, which people worldwide are adopting independently due to the way technology works, Berlin / Shanghai, 2018.
p. 24 / p.25 Those are actually grilled dogs, photographed in the far north of Vietnam. What is right, what is wrong? They eat dogs in China (or Vietnam), which is shocking to us, while we eat pigs, which is unimaginable for Muslims. We like to eat a great steak, while in India the killing of a holy cow was punishable by death until recently. Right or wrong? What's considered normal or abnormal is more often than not based on our own definition of normal. It's not that the Chinese have odd eating habits, but our perception that makes these eating habits appear strange. Just like a Muslim can't understand how we can eat pigs, which he believes to be unclean animals. It is all a matter of perspective and learned truths. Vietnam, 2014.
p. 27 Two times *ONE WAY*, New York City, 2016.
p. 28 / p. 29 Examples of two completely different ways of thinking / living, both Berlin, 2018.
p. 30 / p. 31 The light and its shadow often create unique shapes. It is a call to appreciate and enjoy them. At the same time, they are often short-lived and therefore also a symbol of the transitoriness of life. Wonderful light effects in a gallery with skylights, Berlin, 2018.
p. 32 / p. 33 The subway story happened exactly as conveyed and demonstrates the unique way children perceive the world. The experience triggered a statement I make from time to time: *I want to regain my childlike naivety.* The eye belongs to seven-year-old Helene, Berlin, 2018.
p. 34 / p. 35 If someone had asked me to paint a half moon I would have laughed, convinced I was capable of carrying out said task with ease. Because, after all, every child can paint a half moon. In Southeast Asia I look up at the sky and see a crescent moon. It looks different than expected. It is turned by ninety degrees. It looks like a smiling mouth instead of the familiar sickle. Time and again I realize how deeply rooted my ideas about the world are and at the same time: how wrong they sometimes are.

It is not difficult to understand why the moon in this part of the world looks different; but not until I saw the inclined half moon did I realize that the moon doesn't necessarily look as I believed it to. Our ideas are informed by our environment, in this case by the place where we grew up. The world looks different elsewhere. This experience can be applied to other areas as well.

Our thoughts are based on rigid thinking patterns, we live with preconceived notions. Too rarely do we question things but instead believe what we're told. We accept that which is portrayed as a given. But the world is not always as we see it.

There was a time when a small group of people was adamant that the world was round like a ball instead of a disc. They were dismissed as mad. A commonly held misconception had emerged. But as long as the majority of people believe the earth to be a disc it's difficult to convince them otherwise. Laos, 2014.

p. 36 / p. 37 *A bird of paradise* riding his bicycle through Berlin, accompanied by his parrots. Isn't it just great to do your own thing?! Sonnenallee, Berlin, 2018.

p. 38 / p. 39 Same same, but different. At first I thought the picture on the left might work well with the picture on page 22. But I wanted to keep the pairing on page 22 / page 23 intact. A few days later during a UDK (University of the Arts) tour the young woman from page 38 came to stand in front of me. Without thinking too much I secretly photographed her. From then on I saw people in leopard print outfits almost every day, both Berlin, 2018.

p. 41 Of course, the picture only shows a section of the painting, Berlin, 2018.

p. 42 / p. 43 An expensive car, important or not? At least for many people still a coveted status symbol, Shanghai, 2018.

p. 45 A view from above, at a vernissage, Berlin, 2016.

p. 46 / p. 47 Loosely based on *The Creation of Adam* by Michelangelo, Berlin, 2018.

p. 48 From my series *Supermodels*, Berlin, 2017.

p. 51 Note the right hand of the mannequin, second-hand shop, Berlin, 2018.

p. 52 / p. 53 Beauty and transience. Left: the flower has a wonderful aesthetic of its own although or precisely because it has wilted. In contrast, the search for and promise of beauty in our omnipresent consumer world, both Berlin, 2014 / 2018.

p. 54 A child on the floor painting during an exhibition, Berlin, 2015.

p. 57 Delightful how the glasses and their shadows create an almost optical illusion. Equally wonderful are the shapes of the drops' shadows cast on the wall, exhibition opening, Berlin, 2016.

p. 58 Streetart by *Space Invader*, New York City, 2016. Copyright Artwork: Space Invador.

p. 60 / p. 61 The people inhabiting a city are responsible for how we perceive that city. Without its inhabitants, it is just a lifeless entity. For example, Kreuzberg appears as hip or creative because exciting people do exciting things there. Just a few decades ago the area was classified as a *Gefärdeter Bezirk* (dangerous quarter), a *no-go area*. Often these neighborhoods become boring as soon as the creative people move out. But who benefits from the cities these days? The people who live there or others? New York City, 2016.

p. 65 Reflection of the façade of an old building on a posh car, Berlin, 2018.

p. 66 / p. 67 The *Berlin Kidz* are young graffiti artists who spray paint the most inaccessible public places like skyscrapers or church spires in their unique style. Here we see a skyscraper at Kottbusser Tor, Berlin, 2018.

P. 68 / p. 69 Left side: a display case no longer in use, a *lost paradise* in southern Italy. The

English translation is missing. It's a German wordplay. Literal translation: it used to be beautiful; figurative translation: it's been great. (German: *Schön war's*). Right side: a plug in India. Siracusa, 2018 / India, 2016.

p. 70 An airplane wing above the clouds, 2017.

p. 72 / p. 73 Left: a train station in China, 2018, Right: street scene, Berlin, 2018.

p. 74 A sleeping man in Shanghai, probably the chauffeur, Shanghai, 2018.

p. 76 The album cover *Love Life* by the band *Berlin*, bought in Brooklyn for $3 as a souvenir of a trip to NYC, photographed together with my record collection at home, Berlin, 2018. Copyright record cover: 1984 The David Geffen Company.

p. 78 / p. 79 There is no direct connection between these images. They are just two beautifully designed products in perfect harmony with each other. Left: an ashtray in Paris. There was a time when objects for the public space were designed to look this fantastic. Right: even the rear of a product can be beautiful, Paris, 2016 / Berlin, 2017.

p. 80 / p. 81 On the one hand the image depicts our permanent *connectivity*, but at the same time shows the growing social isolation of our time. Taken on a subway in Shanghai, Shanghai, 2018.

p. 84 / p. 85 Left: a conversation that actually took place on Tinder. Picture: Right: The picture shows the intimacy between two people but contrary to prevailing role models: the black woman seems to be the stronger sex, he leans against her, she rests her arm protectively on his shoulder. Mauerpark, both Berlin, 2017 / 2018.

p. 86 / p. 87 A few years ago two friends and I were philosophizing about life. Both of them are a little bit older than me. The crucial question was: when is the best time to do what you've always wanted to do? Is it better to build security first or to take advantage of the carefreeness that is typically associated with a younger age? I'll never forget a few key sentences: *You know, I may have money today, but tomorrow I might be poor again. And in the same way, if I'm poor now, I may soon get rich again. Money can be available at any time or not at all. But this moment exists only once. Every moment is unique. Every period of time in our lives is unique.* And the other friend nodded and added, maybe a little wistfully: *I will never be 25 again. I will never be 30 again.*

I found this calendar page in the trash at my grandparent's house. It symbolizes time in several ways. On the one hand as a calendar page in and of itself, on the other hand due to the visible marks on it, and ultimately because of the painted woman as its subject, which in this form is no longer contemporary. Berlin, 2017. Copyright Calendar Page: A/S Minerva Reproduktioner, Copenhagen 1970, Calender Girl - 71 Photo: Flemming Adelson.

p. 88 / p. 89 I get asked this question a lot. Sometimes it's offered up as a statement such as this: *You don't do anything anyways.* It never stops to amaze me because I would describe myself as a very busy person. At the same time it is actually a question that everyone should ask themselves. Again and again.

At the beginning of 2014 I embarked on my personal journey, quit my conventional job and kicked off my *Project Leben* (Life). Admittedly, sometimes even I don't know what I'm doing. But I never get bored. Over time, I created a digital folder with almost 100 GB of data. The screenshot can be seen as visualization of my productivity, screenshot, Berlin, 2018. Copyright screendesign: Apple Inc.

p. 90 / p. 91 Work vs. Life. To me, the picture on the left symbolizes the strict and well-ordered working world, while the picture on the right embodies a free-spirited, individual attitude toward life, Berlin, 2018.

p. 93 I like the abstract component of the picture that does not reveal what the photograph depicts. It is a golden tinsel curtain, photographed from below, Berlin, 2018.

p. 94 / p. 95 Both pictures taken on the same day, at the same event, Berlin, 2018.

p. 96 Artificial limb, the ultimate aid, Berlin, 2018.

p. 98 / p. 99 The *Tiefpunkt* (rock bottom) bar in Neukölln, perhaps a symbol of failure vs. an image of an airplane, symbol of freedom, wanderlust and historically also exclusivity, both Berlin, 2018.

p. 100 / p. 101 In most cases, we associate success with professional success (and hence financial independence). But what is success? In general but also on an individual level? Does success necessarily mean a lot of money? Does being successful equal happiness? Note the woman lying underneath the car and ask yourself the question about success once more, India, 2012.

p. 102 / p. 103 A house front in Leipzig. Apparently, only one owner wanted to renovate his property, Leipzig, 2017.

P. 104 Merda d'artista (Artist's shit), May 1961, tin can, printed paper, $4,8 \times \o 6$ cm, © Fondazione Piero Manzoni. Photo: private collection, New York City, 2016.

p. 106 / p. 107 I meet stressed-out friends, stressed-out from work, and with little time but lots of worries. I notice: a compliment always makes things better. A compliment opens the soul and turns sad faces into happy ones. It quickly became clear to me that I wanted to create a compliment: *And You Look Adorable*. My idea was to make a stamp with which everyone will be able to spread the compliment themselves. In addition, I designed the packaging to reference past times, which were far less fast-paced. It was my very first project. AND YOU LOOK ADORABLE, Berlin, 2014.

p. 108 A man making music under a concrete bridge, Shangahi, 2018.

p. 110 / p. 111 Both pictures symbolize freedom. The houseplants are trapped inside, behind a window. They are juxtaposed another plant growing outside, in front of the window, beneath the open sky. Right: barbed wire, symbol of borders, barriers, exclusions. In the blurred background you can see blue sky with a few small scattered clouds. A traditional synonym for freedom, both Berlin, 2018.

p. 113 Young woman with very short hair, Mauerpark, Berlin, 2018.

p. 114 / p. 115 BVG bus stop request display STOP + cmd+C (Apple key combination for copy) = Stop Copying. An appeal: create your own work. Everything in the world looks increasingly the same (see following page), informed by the uniform styles of Instagram and Pinterest. Isn't it boring if every place ends up looking the same? Whether in New York, Berlin or Shanghai, the same sight everywhere, sometimes down to the very last detail, both Berlin, 2018.

p. 116 / p. 117 Both pictures look practically the same: a medicine bottle used as vase, a star-shaped flower, a silver car in the background. But the pictures were taken in two entirely different parts of the world, (see description above), Hong Kong / Berlin, 2018.

p. 118 / 119 *Blind Old Man*, photograph from the series *Digital Portraits*. An elderly gentleman on the Paris subway. He looks different, stylish, he obviously isn't mainstream. He's holding his cell phone in his hand but needs a magnifying glass to read the display. The magnifying glass is a tool from the analog world. But he's using it to operate modern technology. The analog and digital worlds become one for him. In this respect we could also ask ourselves: what is our approach to dealing with modern technology?

But it's not only a picture of a man on the subway, in fact, it is a photograph of a monitor displaying the picture with the gentleman as it's being edited in Photoshop. On the right hand side you can see the tool palette. Interestingly, the programmers took their cues from the familiar analog world and named the tools accordingly: a wrench, a stamp, a folder. The tools were named after things we know. The analog world became digitized. Today, computers are increasingly taking on a life of their own. Algorithms are based on pattern recognition. All we do is feed them our data. Many programs once written are self-learning and develop autonomously. But to what end?

At the top of the picture in the middle you can see the *help* button. With the introduction of computers came the help button. *I call for help!* In a literal sense something we do when in danger. I can't do it by myself, I need help. Using the computer, the program exceeds my capabilities. But this button is gradually disappearing. Artificial intelligence takes its place and help can only be found somewhere buried deep in the confusing settings. Paris 2016 / Berlin 2017.

p. 120 / S. 121 Light pollution, we can no longer see the stars because of all the light sources on earth. The red sky is created by the reflections of the city's neon lamps, China, 2018.

p. 122 / p. 123 Question the world. Nothing has to be the way it is. Trolley from above at Tegel airport, Berlin, 2018.

p. 124 / p. 125 At least in the picture something is missing, presumably a statue, Berlin, 2018.

p. 126 / p. 127 Forget fear. Smile and say hello. Inspired by Anaïs Nin's words: *Anxiety is love's greatest killer,* Berlin, 2016.

p. 128 / p. 129 Hate vs. Love. Front door in Neukölln, vernissage in Kreuzberg, both Berlin, 2018.

p. 130 / 131 Shapes of perversity. I took both pictures independently of each other. In both cases it was not obvious to me what they might represent. Not until the evening, while cropping and rotating the pictures on my computer screen, came this pair to light. By the way, the image on the right is old paint coming off the wall of a house, Berlin, 2018.

p. 133 A typical night in a bar, Berlin, 2013.

p. 134 / p. 135 Left: *Light explosion* on a wall, right: light and shadow on my ceiling, both Berlin, 2018.

p. 136 / p. 137 The quote is not just about the dogs of Delhi. It also refers to our ways of thinking and living that we are often trapped in, Red Fort, Delhi, 2016.

p. 138 Paris, 2017.

p. 140 / p. 141 The two sentences describe two contrasting ways of living. Photo: metal grid on the High Line NYC. An almost abstract picture emerges. The combination of light and metal creates this unique play of colors, New York City, 2016.

p. 142 / p. 143 Left: the stripes were generated by light, shadow, heating pipes and color reflections from my exterior facade. An appeal to notice and relish small pleasures and appreciate them. Right: the cab has the color of my house. The two images work amazingly well together because of their matching colors, no hidden deeper meaning, both Berlin, 2018.

p. 144 Rainy scenery, Macau, 2018.

p. 147 A manhole cover just like any other in Berlin. We walk across it on a daily basis but overlook the screaming face, Berlin, 2018.

p. 148 / p. 149 Tragic pub scene. The apparently sorrow-stricken girl has placed her cell phone on her beer glass and drunkenly plays with it. Only a few photos show sadness or despair as clearly as this one, which is why it is one of my favorites despite its poor quality, Kreuzberg, Berlin, 2016.

p. 150 / p. 151 A beautiful picture even though the bus is old and run-down. The picture depicts the beauty of ugliness. Regarding the quote: what we consider to be true also depends on how we define truth or what we believe in. India, 2016.

p. 152 / p. 153 We tend to overlook the light, this miracle of nature, far too often. A reminder to appreciate the little things in life and an appeal to open our eyes, Berlin, 2018.

p. 154 / p. 155 A sentence that can be read in several ways. Is the art not being content with anything or is the art being content without possessions? Berlin, 2018.

p. 157 A young woman in China, China, 2018.

p. 158 / p. 159 Left: tattoo of a maybe 18-year-old Chinese boy in work clothes. Right: overlapping cameras in front of the terracotta warriors in China. The two pages depict the everyday struggle to find images and the demand for *likes* on social media, both China, 2018.

p. 160 / p. 161 We spend far too much time planning our future instead of living in the now. *You are here,* Airport, Shanghai, 2018.

p. 162 The picture doesn't reveal the actual object that was photographed and hence spurs our creativity. It is the core of an old mattress in the streets of Berlin, 2018.

p. 164 / p. 165 Serendipity, my first *Conceptual Photograph*, more information at www.felixsandberg.de/serendipity , published as an edition, Berlin, 2016 / 2017.

p. 166 / p. 167 Cities are considered to be efficient, i. e., the more people per square meter, the more efficient a city. But what about meaningfulness? What about quality of life? Should urban planning be based solely on efficiency criteria? Hong Kong at night, one of the most densely populated cities in the world, Hong Kong, 2018.

p. 169 Spiky cones on the handrail between two escalators, so that no one uses it as a slide. The picture symbolizes an *evil city*, Berlin, 2018.

p. 170 / p. 171 In a way the hand's shape resembles that of the mountains. In addition, the colors of the subway station and those of the sunset in the mountains are almost identical. Nevertheless, it is a pair of opposites: city vs. nature. Berlin, 2018 / Himalaya, India, 2016.

p. 172 A mural by *JR* in New York City, 2016, Copyright Artwork: JR.

p. 174 / p. 175 Left: cramped living conditions. In contrast, the imprisoned fish from the *Goldfish Market,* which the locals like to keep in their small apartments. A nice analogy for our own existence, Hong Kong, 2018.

p. 176 / p. 177 The pictures perfectly complement each other, yet are also a pair of opposites. On the left hand side, depicting nature's magic, a giant drop of water *floats* on a leaf vs. a lonely city on the right, with hectic people staring at their cell phones. The colors in both pictures are similar but in the city stem from artificial light, both China, 2018.

p. 178 / p. 179 Time or status symbol? It's a matter of attitude toward life. Graffiti in Neukölln, Berlin, 2017.

p. 180 Yes, that's my belly indeed but it's deliberately staged to look unattractive. Today, of course, I'm in much better shape, Berlin, 2018.

p. 182 / p. 183 Left: the view from my window. Right: the surveillance camera of a Berlin-based entrepreneur, facing Torstrasse, Berlin, 2018.

p. 184 / S. 185 Both pictures depict mobility in general; both the car-friendly city and the shiny car stand for unnecessary energy consumption and as such reveal absurd ways of human thinking. In addition, they harmonize due to the counter-rotating *curve* that appears in both pictures. Right: I am fascinated by the flowing shapes of the reflections created by the angular design of the fender. In some ways they are reminiscent of a psychedelic picture, Shanghai / Berlin, 2018.

p. 187 Thanks to the cameras and smartphones the main *attraction* in the picture can't be seen. Sitting in the car is the Dalai Lama, India, 2016.

p. 188 / 189 A devilish car, Shanghai, 2018.

p. 190 Probably the most remote region I have ever visited. High up in the Himalayas, in an area that can only be reached on foot, I was only the second person from the western world the children of a cashmere farmer had ever met. At first extremely shy they then started playing with my camera and proceeded to show me their goats, staged themselves with them and wanted to be photographed again and again and again, India, 2016.

p. 192 / p. 193 Technical failure. Left: Transrapid in Shanghai. The former technological flagship is getting old, the seats are worn out, the handles scuffed. A groundbreaking technological concept, which due to unfortunate circumstances didn't succeed. On the right: an iPhone, a pioneer of our contemporary technological environment, but even that is not *infallible*. The display is smashed, the home button no longer works and has to be controlled via the internal app. But the screen has a wonderfully golden glow because of the picture being displayed, Shanghai / Berlin, 2018.

p. 194 / p. 195 The algorithm of iPhoto tries to assign names to the faces of the terracotta warriors. Since it can't find a comparable person in my database, it labels them *Unbenannt* (unnamed). The software does not recognize that the terracotta worriers aren't human. An example of a failing algorithm, Berlin, 2018, Screenshot from iPhoto, Copyright iPhoto: Apple Inc.

p. 196 / p. 197 Inspired by *Nietzsche's* prolog from *Thus spoke Zarathustra: One must still have chaos in oneself to be able to give birth to a dancing star,* Berlin, 2019.

p. 198 / p. 199 Food to go. Right: a girl snacks on chicken feet on a high-speed train in China. She is wearing very light plastic gloves, which are disposed of after eating, so she doesn't need to wash her hands. Berlin / China, 2018.

p. 200 / p. 201 The statement refers to seemingly simple things like paintings by Jackson Pollock or works by Martin Creed, Berlin, 2018.

p. 202 Four letters on my window sill. They together built the word NEIN, which means *no* in German, Berlin, 2019.

p. 205 New York City, 2016.

p. 207 Construction site of the new Axel Springer building, Berlin, 2018.

p. 208 / p. 209 Most statements convey opinions, rarely facts. Nevertheless, opinions are often discussed as if they were facts. *If we have data, let's look at data. If all we have are opinions, let's go with mine.* - Jim F. Barksdale. Photo: sky without any added filter, Southeast Asia, 2015.

p. 210 / p. 211 I am impressed by the salmon. It swims halfway around the world only to return home again. It doesn't seem to make sense. It simply lives its life, driven by its instincts, Canada, 2006.

p. 212 / p. 213 Happiness is omnipresent in today's consumer and advertising world: buy something and be happy. But the picture shows nothing but emptiness, exudes no coziness, anything but a happy living environment. Yet for many, a contemporary privately owned home with large windows is a particularly desirable aim of life, Berlin, 2018.

p. 214 / p. 215 Notice the little joys in life, like a power outlet in Copenhagen, 2017.

p. 216 *We deserve to be happy.* Berlin, 2018.

p. 218 / p. 219 *Little Black Box.* A box in which to store all your wishes, ideas, dreams or things you want to leave behind. Choose wisely because once you close the box, it's closed forever. More information: www.felixsandberg.de/little-black-box , Berlin, 2016.

p. 221 Paris from above, Paris, 2017.

p. 222 / p. 223 In general: treasure the things you take for granted, Baltic Sea, 2018.

p. 225 A dry leaf. I am fascinated by the stem's *grooves,* Siracusa, 2018.

p. 226 / p. 227 Similar to how we relish rays of sun after a cold winter (see p. 224), the completion of a project can make us happy as well. It is a great feeling. The greater the struggle, the greater the sense of achievement afterwards. Creating something, no matter of what kind, is never easy. The deprivation, the time spent, the frustration, the invested capital, the sweat, it takes a lot to achieve a goal. Precisely because it is difficult, not everyone tries to or succeeds in doing it. That is exactly why compliments such as *great!, beautiful!, impressive!* or, ideally, the selling of our creation, means getting recognition. If it weren't hard work, it would be normal and not perceived as something special, neither by the outside world nor ourselves. A cactus on my window-sill. It sometimes hurts me as well but that is what makes it special, Berlin, 2016.

p. 228 Two cows cuddled up, India, 2016.

p. 231 Bar in Neukölln, I like the surreal component the mask on the table adds, Berlin, 2014.

p. 233 A wall in the way. Example of the absurdity of human activity, Shanghai, 2018.

p. 235 The picture was taken on a bus in China. The driver, having a job that probably does get dull from time to time, had placed two small plants on the front shelf, right next to the doors. He obviously took care of them and in turn they gave him and the passengers some pleasure, China, 2018.

p. 236 / p. 237 *Serendipity II*, Paris / Berlin, 2017.

p. 239 Another jazz concert on this trip, very experimental, with the sunset in the background making it one of the most beautiful experiences of that year, New York City, 2016.

p. 240 Macau, 2018.

p. 242 Today's trends are moving so fast that sometimes you don't know if what you laid out the night before is still *in* the next day. The clothes worn by hipsters today, which some people might make fun of, often become mainstream a short time later. By then, most people will already have forgotten that they used to make them laugh, Weissensee School of Art, Berlin, 2018.

p. 245 Mural in New York City, quote and picture taken from Moodboard New York City, www.felixsandberg.de/moodboard-nyc , NYC, 2016.

p. 246 / p. 247 Shit happens, take it easy, Berlin, 2018 / New York City, 2016.

p. 248 / p. 249 Sometimes you are just not in control. Success or failure (whatever that is) is often a matter of chance. You can be too early, too late or in the right place at the right time. You can't really influence it. A friend of mine works at a large consumer goods manufacturer. With the same resources such as manpower, agencies and so on, half of the products sell and the other half doesn't; nobody knows why. I could hardly have set up this picture, it was pure chance, Berlin, 2016.

p. 250 / p. 251 An older gentleman is sitting on the *Tempelhofer Feld* (former airport, now a park) playing his accordion and watching the sunset. How wonderful. Quote: Charles Eames. Left: a leather outfit for particular sexual preferences. Whatever your pleasures, take them seriously, Berlin, 2018.

p. 252 Mattress on the streets of Neukölln, probably sprayed spontaneously, Berlin, 2017.

p. 254 / p. 255 My streetart project *Money Makes Me Happy*. Only after the copper has oxidized does the smiley face become visible, Berlin, 2017.

p. 256 / p. 257 There is hardly anything in the world that everybody likes to the same extent. And that's completely ok. A *no* doesn't necessarily mean that the quality of your work isn't up to scratch. Maybe it just not to that person's taste, but many others may like it. I've asked many shops to sell my products and often they said no. But at the same time a lot of people were enthusiastic about my creations. I have approached many bloggers and asked them to write about me, but they didn't. Others, however, did so without me asking them. A *no* is part of the (creative) process. There are always people who will say no. Accept this without doubting your abilities, believe in yourself and pursue your dreams, Berlin, 2018.

p. 258 / p. 259 I don't know what to write about these pictures but I think they look really good together. Left: reflections on the street. I don't know where they came from but they were clearly reflections. None of the other passers-by noticed this wonderful play of colors. Right: vintage Mercedes in Tegel, Berlin, 2018.

p. 260 One evening while walking down the street with friends I discovered the shadow of a little man on the door of a portable toilet on a construction site. I was thrilled, my friends laughed at me. I saw the shadow of a little man and was fascinated by this wonderful spectacle. The shadow was still visible when a few hours later on my way home I passed the construction site again. Even though it was the middle of the night, I went home to get my camera and photographed the little guy. The next evening he was gone. This picture is the only evidence of an inspiring night. What do you see in this picture? Berlin, 2016.

p. 262 / p. 263 Agonizing over which socks to wear today, Berlin, 2017.

p. 265 A bus station waiting room in China, 2018.

p. 266 Wonderful nature creates unique shapes again and again. Here it is an octopus – at least I can see it, Berlin, 2016.

p. 268 - p. 271 *Rise and Shine*, find more information at: www.felixsandberg.de/rise-and-shine , Berlin, 2015.

p. 298 - p. 301 A parody of the unnecessarily complicate artwork labels found at exhibitions. Picture: family photo, southern Germany 1988 / Berlin 2016.

p. 303 Self-portrait using a mirror, taken with the last picture of the film after photographing the series *Supermodels*. Specks of dust and scratches are visible. The decision not to retouch the image completely was a nod to the analog technique I used. I like this picture a lot because you can clearly see the exhaustion at the end of the day but at the same time how relaxed and happy I am due to what I have accomplished, Berlin, 2018.

Tinderama

My shortest Tinder date lasted less than four minutes, most of which were spent waiting, and cost me €2. The 43 minutes it took me to get there and back home are not included in the calculation. But I got some flambéed ribs for free. They were leftovers. The remains. My date had barbecued them. They were very good.

Match.

Hey! Have you managed to escape the heat? I text her because today is a very hot day. She: *No, I have to work. Do you want to come round later?*

This spontaneous invitation overwhelms me. Exhausted after a lengthy bike ride I'm lying on my couch and can't imagine wanting to thrill a woman. Not even verbally. I ask her what she does for a living, and she answers frying fries and spareribs. Today she's working on the fries. Well, that sounds great, I think to myself. She texts back that I can think about it. After doing exactly that, I cancel. Fatigue, doubt and laziness have gained the upper hand. But since I am still interested, the next day I try to persuade her to meet up. She is working again. This time on the ribs. She asks me to stop by. Thoughts are running through my head. A date at the grill restaurant? What exactly is it that she does there? Is it even possible to talk to her there? And what does she imagine an after-work date to be like? After working the grill for eight hours the distinct smell of barbecue will have settled in her hair and clothes – does she intend to go out like that? Will we be sitting at a bar like that? Or will we go to her place first, so she can take a shower and then move on? Either way, it's a strange meeting with a stranger. Or will we have a beer at her workplace, where she knows everyone? Does she always invite men to pick her up? What will the other employees think when they see me? *Ah, another one?* I reply that I will drop by later.

I pass some time with running errands and then text her to ask if now is a good time. *Yes, of course! Just come by!* So I hit the road. By bike because the weather is nice. While I'm still on my way, my cell phone hums; I am shocked by what I read: she suggests I better bring someone along because she won't have much time to chat. Where am I supposed to get company now? So I tell her that I'd rather come by later in the evening. And thus I enjoy a spontaneous bike ride through summery Berlin. The last sun of the day illuminates the urban canyon. I let my thoughts run, chill in a nice spot by the canal, enjoy the sunset, ride back to Neukölln, get a sandwich from the Turkish shop and at home drop onto the couch, completely wiped out. My cell phone hums, and she writes: *Whatever, just come by now.* I take a moment to think about it. *All right*, I text back. This is a unique opportunity. Apparently, she really wants to see me. This time I take the S-Bahn. It's crazy how crowded the train is on a Sunday evening. These people look pretty exhausted, I think to myself. Many of them. I am relaxed.

Then I receive another message from her. M*aybe we should rather meet on Wednesday. It'll be less hassle.* I absorb the news. Since I have just reached my destination, I text back: *I just arrived in Friedrichshain. I am going to stop by for a moment. We can check each other out and then decide if we want to meet up again on Wednesday in a more relaxed atmosphere.*

To enter the premises where she works I have to pay an entrance fee of €2. After handing over the cash I go in and immediately see her. Of course, in real life she looks a bit different than in the pictures. That's pretty common. I believe I do look the way I do in pictures.

She looks in my direction without recognizing me, turns around, and looks at me again. Now that she realizes it's me, a smile lights up her face, and she reaches out to greet me. I am facing a breathtakingly odd but at the same time beautiful image: she's standing there, attractive, smiling, with her arms wide open dressed in a long black rubber apron, which is filthy and dripping with fat, aspic or BBQ sauce. I can't tell exactly what it is. It's probably a mix of all three. Maybe I seem irritated, because now she examines her outfit and says that perhaps she shouldn't hug me the way she looks. I reply that it is okay and simply say hello.

We talk briefly. *I just have to clean up real quick, and then we can leave.* A guy, presumably her boss, turns around and in a low voice that's still loud enough not to be ignored snaps at her: *I need you here for at least another two hours, you know that, right?* At that, she turns to me, smiles, hands me a plateful of ribs and explains that it's probably not going to work out that day but that I should have the spareribs. I am thrilled, ribs for free. I hide my disappointment, warmly thank her, enjoy the fried goods and say goodbye to my date soon after. Unfortunately, I never saw that great woman again.

I can't remember the title

I spend a free afternoon with friends and do the most fatal thing I possibly could do in that situation. I look at my cell phone and check my mails. *Ping.* There it is. It's a mail, which I no longer expected at that time. I read it and it destroys my mood for the next couple of days. About a year ago I had the idea of writing this book. Now the layout is set, the selection of pictures is final and all texts are edited in both languages. My editorial deadline was more than four weeks ago and actually the book should has been printed weeks ago but there were some delays in the production process. And now this mail reaches me. It is a mail of a Parisian gallery owner. A couple of weeks ago I had written to him and asked for his consent to use a story, which took place in his gallery. I had already taken out any reference to him or his gallery, but now he asked me to omit the story entirely. There couldn´t be any bigger frustration. What was particularly annoying was the fact, that I not only had lost one of my favorite stories, but also that I now had to rework many parts of the book. The easiest way would be to keep the layout as it was and to just exchange the aforesaid story with another one. But which one should I use? I still had some stories in my archive, but the simple exchange with a new story somehow didn´t feel right. I liked the idea of leaving the pages blank, but without any further explanation this would have caused more confusion I think.

Now, instead, here is this text about the loss of a story, which is a small insight into something that normally remains hidden. At the same time, this story shows the challenges and disappointments, which are somewhat part of the (creative) process.

The picture on page 202 shows four letters on top of each other. If you look closely, you can see that they form the word *NEIN*, which means *no* in German.

A salmon's purpose in life

The life of a salmon seems like a constant battle, fraught with danger and pain. From an external point of view it seems almost pointless but for this very reason also uniquely fascinating.

A salmon is born in a body of water in the Alaskan high mountains. Newly hatched, its instincts drive it to embark on a long journey through countless streams and rivers. It is still small, measuring only a few centimeters. Its destination is the nutrient-rich ocean water. On its journey it encounters many dangers, particularly as it's such a small fish. Nevertheless, it continues to migrate, always further, until it reaches its destination. Once arrived, it feeds as much as possible and stays put for a few years. It feeds and grows and feeds and grows. Its singular goal is to gain as much fat as possible to build up enough energy for the swim back. Back to the high mountains, to exactly the same place it came from. Back to the river, stream or pond where it was born. Guided by intuition and its instincts, it finds its way home – as inconceivable as it may be, traveling several thousand kilometers. But this route is anything but easy. It fights its way over rocks, swims upstream in raging rivers, against the current, uphill. It overcomes rapids and cliffs. Again and again, it gets swept away by the current. But it does not give up, jumps high out of the water, hits a rock and is washed downstream again. But it does not give up, tries again, countless times, again, again and again, until it overcomes the obstacle. Occasionally, it will rest to recover. But even that is not without danger. Bears know about the all-you-can-eat buffet and lurk along the way to fish for the migrating salmon. Quite a few get caught by bears and their remains fertilize the forests of Alaska. Those who survive continue to migrate until they finally reach the waters of their birth. By the time they get there the ordeal has left visible scars. They are emaciated and their bodies battered and bruised. But they have made it and accomplish their last, perhaps only task: the females spawn, the males fertilize the eggs. Immediately afterwards the female dies. The males guard the eggs for a while and then die as well. A few months later the offspring hatches and the cycle starts again.

Little moment – you are simply awesome!

A journey through New York at night kicks off in an old red Honda. We take the East Side Highway to Harlem. I look at the skyline. You can see office buildings and the million-dollar-view skyscrapers. On many floors the lights are already on or still on, and I wonder why. It's a peaceful ride. I'm daydreaming and enjoying myself very much. I am traveling with a young woman. She is the driver of the nippy little red car. On the back seat there's a frying pan. I ask her what that's all about. She says she is in the process of moving house.

We visit a jazz bar in Harlem. One of those places I like to call an honest place. The bar has grown organically instead of having been a design project. Honest places usually tell a story, often from a different time. Honest places are alive. The doorman greets us with a friendly smile and opens his door for us. We enter. Almost all seats are filled. We are led to a small table near the stage. It is dark and the drinks menu manageable. I decide to go for a classic drink. The music is loud and our conversation low key. I observe the other guests. They made an attempted at dressing up. It's obvious. All black gentlemen wear hats. Even inside. I'm also wearing a hat, I'm also keeping it on. I watch the musicians. Their faces are like an open book. Revealing everything. The drummer plays a solo and his face is testimony to his joy. The faster he plays, the more impressive his facial expressions. His eyes are closed. In a trance-like state he floats through his solo, just like we float through the night. Meanwhile, the man at the piano keeps an eye on everything. He is the bandleader. He watches the audience and notices everything. Is someone asleep, is someone enjoying himself or herself or is the bartender too noisily shaking his ice cubes? He hears everything. And he reacts to all of it with the way he plays or moves his body, with a little nod or the shaking of his head. And after the music stopped, the applause died down and the drinks were finished, we sit again in her red sports car and glide on through the night.

Es braucht einen gewissen Grad an Solipsismus, um Künstler zu sein

Das Bild *Es braucht einen gewissen Grad an Solipsismus, um Künstler zu sein* (vorherige Seite) zeigt den Künstler in einer sehr frühen Schaffensphase, aufgenommen bei der Performance *Waffel und Puderzucker – sinnliche Blicke, unattraktive Badegäste*.

Schockiert von den vielfältigen Erscheinungsbildern leicht bis unbekleideter Badegäste stellte sich der Künstler die für ihn zentrale Frage, wie ein natürlicher Formprozess diese absurd, teils surreal, manchmal gar abstoßend hässlich anmutenden Formen geschaffen haben kann. Schnell erkannte er, dass diese fremdartigen Gestalten Ergebnisse natürlicher Prozesse sind, die durch gezielte Aktionen, wie beispielsweise durch mehr oder mindere Zufuhr ausgewählter chemischer Substanzen natürlicher Basis, direkt steuerbar sind.

In visionärer Weise verwendete der Künstler fortan kristalline Energieträger in pulverisierter Form als gestalterisches Element.

Die verführerischen Blicke wirken anziehend und verstörend zugleich. Dass sie gespielt sind, merken viele Betrachter erst bei längerem Hinschauen. Nicht wenige erwidern die Blicke unreflektiert und glauben darin nihilistische Botschaften zu erkennen.

Eingesperrt in seiner frühkünstlerischen Naivität wählte er bald darauf nichts Geringeres als seinen eigenen Körper als bevorzugtes Medium. Er experimentierte exzessiv und über Jahre hinweg, was in messbarem Übergewicht und damit spätpubertären Hänseleien ihm gegenüber endete.

Auch diese Performance beweist wiederholt, dass der Künstler seiner Zeit regelmäßig weit voraus war, was die aktuelle Debatte über übergewichtige Kinder und Jugendliche schmerzhaft beweist. Die Performance ist als Meilenstein bei der Auseinandersetzung mit dem Thema zu betrachten. Vergleiche mit Beuys oder Abramović liegen nahe und sind seitens des Künstlers durchaus gewollt.

Die heutige Würdigung seines Schaffens ist schwierig. Die Werke des Künstlers befinden sich weder im MOMA noch im MOCA. Auch große Galerien haben nie Interesse an seinen Werken bekundet. Genauso wenig sind sie in nennenswerten Privatsammlungen aufzufinden. Ein Großteil seines Werkes hat sich in den letzten Jahren ohnehin in Luft aufgelöst. Auf tragikomische Weise bestätigt dies jedoch auch seine Genialität.

Als Performancekünstler scheut er sich ohnehin davor, im Museum wie ein Tier im Zoo, ausgestellt zu werden. Er möchte lieber seine Freiheit ausleben.

Auf die Anerkennung seines Gesamtwerkes wartet der Künstler bis heute vergebens. Der Künstler lebt und arbeitet in seiner eigenen Welt. Anzutreffen ist er meistens in Berlin.

To be an artist you need a certain degree of solipsism

The picture *To be an artist you need a certain degree of solipsism* (previous page) shows the artist in a very early creative phase. *It was taken during the performance waffles and powdered sugar – sensuous glances, unattractive bathers.*

Shocked by the manifold appearances of lightly dressed to undressed bathers, the artist asked himself the central question: how could a natural shaping process have created these absurd, partly surreal, sometimes even repulsively ugly shapes? He quickly realized that these strange shapes are the result of natural processes that can be directly controlled by specific actions, such as supplying bigger or smaller amounts of selected nature-based chemical substances.

In a visionary manner, the artist henceforth used crystalline sources of energy in pulverized form as a design element.

The seductive glances come across as both attractive and disturbing. It takes many viewers a while to realize that it's all just an act. Quite a few instinctively return the looks and believe them to convey nihilistic messages.

Trapped in his early artistic naivety, he soon chose nothing less than his own body as his preferred medium. After years of excessive experiments, he became measurably overweight and thus the target of adolescent teasing.

Again, this performance demonstrates that the artist frequently was far ahead of his time, which the current debate on obesity in children and adolescents painfully demonstrates. The performance is to be regarded as a milestone in dealing with the issue. Comparisons with Beuys or Abramović come to mind and are intended by the artist.

The appreciation of his artistic work in the present proves difficult. The artist's works are on display neither in the MOMA nor the MOCA. Large galleries have also failed to express any interest in them. Just like they can't be found among any of the significant private collections. Besides, a large part of his work has vanished into thin air in recent years. In a tragicomic way, however, this also confirms his genius.

As a performance artist, he is afraid of being on display in a museum like a zoo animal anyway. He would rather enjoy his freedom.

To this day, the artist is still waiting for the recognition of his body of work. The artist lives and works in his own world. Most of the time he can be found in Berlin.

Schreibt mir gerne:
hello@felixsandberg.de

Besucht auch meine Website:
www.felixsandberg.de

Vielen Dank an alle, die mich bei diesem Projekt unterstützt haben und mir konstruktiven Input gaben. Besonderer Dank gilt: Helene Herzog, Lisa Kober, Claudius Römer, Peter Sandberg, Hector Santillan, Benjamin Schmid, Ina Schneider, Vivian Schröder und Helene, Falk Straube, Daniela Vogt.

Feel free to say hi:
hello@felixsandberg.de

Please visit my website:
www.felixsandberg.de

Many thanks to everyone who supported me throughout this project and offered constructive input. Special thanks to: Helene Herzog, Lisa Kober, Claudius Römer, Peter Sandberg, Hector Santillan, Benjamin Schmid, Ina Schneider, Vivian Schröder und Helene, Falk Straube, Daniela Vogt.

Impressum

Veröffentlicht von Felix Sandberg
Mareschstr. 12, 12055 Berlin, Germany
www.felixsandberg.de

Fotos, Text, Gestaltung inkl. Cover: Felix Sandberg
Lektorat Deutsch: Ramona Ramtke
Lektorat Englisch: Ela Kremer

1. Auflage
Gedruckt in Lettland

© Felix Sandberg 2019
Alle Teile dieses Buches unterliegen dem Urheberrecht und dürfen nicht ohne schriftliche Genehmigung des Urhebers in irgendeiner Form vervielfältigt oder verbreitet werden.

ISBN: 978-3-00-062533-6

Imprint

Published by Felix Sandberg
Mareschstr. 12, 12055 Berlin, Germany
www.felixsandberg.de

Photos, text, design incl. cover: Felix Sandberg
Copy editing German: Ramona Ramtke
Copy editing English: Ela Kremer

1st Edition
Printed in Latvia

© Felix Sandberg 2019
All parts of this book are subject to copyright and other intellectual property rights and may not be used, reproduced or distributed in any form or by any means without the author's written consent.

ISBN: 978-3-00-062533-6